FIGHTING
WORDS

FIGHTING WORDS

Personal
Essays by Black
Gay Men

EDITED BY CHARLES MICHAEL SMITH

AVON BOOKS ◆ NEW YORK

Pages 181–182 constitute an extension of
this copyright page.

AVON BOOKS, INC.
1350 Avenue of the Americas
New York, New York 10019

Copyright © 1999 by Charles Michael Smith
Cover photograph by Russ Quackenbush Photography
Published by arrangement with the editor
Library of Congress Catalog Card Number: 99-94861
ISBN: 0-380-79947-2
www.avonbooks.com

First Avon Books Trade Paperback Printing: June 1999

AVON TRADEMARK REG. U.S. PAT. OFF. AND IN OTHER COUNTRIES, MARCA REGISTRADA,
HECHO EN U.S.A.

Printed in the U.S.A.

OPM   10 9 8 7 6 5 4 3 2 1

EDITOR'S NOTE

The idea of doing the book you now hold in your hands originated with my friend, the late Assotto Saint (aka Yves Lubin), who was the founder and publisher of Galiens Press in New York City. (The name Galiens was the combination of the words "gay" and "aliens"; both Assotto and his lover, Jan, were foreign-born—Assotto was from Haiti, Jan was from Sweden.)

For several years I dreamed of editing a black gay male anthology of short fiction to fill a woeful void in American gay literature. Assotto with great wisdom and insight suggested that I do an essay anthology instead. He felt it best suited me because of my extensive background in print journalism. He even offered to publish it himself. Sadly, not long after, Assotto, who had full-blown AIDS, became too ill to publish *Words of Fire*, the project's title at that time. However, I am forever grateful to Assotto for providing me the opportunity to publish an anthology and for believing in my abilities as a writer and editor.

I am also grateful to my former editor Charlotte Abbott. By acquiring this book for Avon Books, she proved that she saw value in it.

ACKNOWLEDGMENTS

The following essays were originally published in a slightly different form:

Joseph F. Beam, "Brother to Brother: Words From the Heart," *The New York Native*, October 22–November 4, 1984 (Issue #101).

Rodney Christopher, "Becoming a Movement," *BLK* magazine, January 1991.

Mark Haile, "I Pay the Black Tax," *Square Peg* magazine, June 1992.

Mark Haile, "The Truth about Stonewall," *BLK* magazine, June 1989.

Essex Hemphill, "I Am a Homosexual," in "Say, Brother" column, *Essence* magazine, November 1983.

R. Leigh (Tré) Johnson, "Kissing Cousin," *The James White Review*, Summer 1993.

Kheven L. LaGrone, "Beneath the Veneer," *SBC* magazine, November/December 1992 (Vol. 1, #4).

Rodney McCoy, Jr., "Breaking Silence in the Middle of a Holocaust, *JFY* Magazine, Vol. 1, #4 (1993).

Bruce Morrow, "Confronting Adversity," originally entitled "Black and Gay: A High-Wire Act," *The New York Times* ("The City" section), November 6, 1994.

•

To Yves F. Lubin (a.k.a. Assotto Saint), 1957–1994

I will write words of fire
that tell the truths you dare to deny
that speak of faggotry
that herald brothers loving brothers
sisters loving sisters
fiercely, (proudly)
without remorse

—from the poem "This Snap's for You!"
 by Fabian Thomas

CONTENTS

ESSAY EXCERPTS
XV

INTRODUCTION
1

I • IDENTITY

DREADLOCKS
Mark Simmons
9

BENEATH THE VENEER
Kheven L. LaGrone
13

**FEAR OF A GAY IDENTITY:
A PERSONAL ACCOUNT ON INTERNALIZING HETEROSEXISM**
Geoffrey Giddings
17

**COLORING OUTSIDE THE LINES:
AN ESSAY AT DEFINITION**
Reginald Shepherd
24

THOUGHTS ON TRADE/ENDING AN OBSESSION
Edwin L. Greene
35

BROTHER TO BROTHER:
WORDS FROM THE HEART
Joseph F. Beam
42

II • RELATIONSHIPS

MENTORING GAY YOUTH
Thom Bean
49

I HATE BASKETBALL
Kevin McGruder
54

GIL'S STORY
Sur Rodney (Sur)
57

BEHIND THESE PRISON WALLS
Eugene Harris
63

CLOSETS
G. Winston James
67

KISSING COUSIN
R. Leigh (Tré) Johnson
72

LIKE THE WHITE GIRLS
Tod A. Roulette
78

THE LETTER
Donald Keith Jackson
83

LOOKING FOR LOVE
Jalal
88

III • FACING THE AIDS CRISIS

BREAKING SILENCE IN THE MIDDLE OF A HOLOCAUST
Rodney McCoy, Jr.
97
THE OTHER ORPHANS
Robert E. Penn
101
STAYING HEALTHY IN THE AGE OF AIDS
Arnold Jackson
107

IV • RACISM AND HOMOPHOBIA

DEAREST BROTHER SET
Conrad R. Pegues
113
I PAY THE BLACK TAX
Mark Haile
124
CONFRONTING ADVERSITY
Bruce Morrow
128
WHY I'M NOT MARCHING
David Frechette
131
PROJECT ERASURE
Fabian Thomas
134
**THE EMERGENCE OF AN AFRICAN
GAY AND LESBIAN COMMUNITY**
Cary Alan Johnson
138
SOME OF MY WORDS
Lawrence Dewyatt Abrams
144

A PLACE AT THE ALTAR
Lynwoodt Jenkins
147
I AM A HOMOSEXUAL
Essex Hemphill
150

V • LEGACY

BECOMING A MOVEMENT
Rodney Christopher
155
THE TRUTH ABOUT STONEWALL
Mark Haile
164

CONTRIBUTORS
172

ESSAY EXCERPTS

SOME OF MY WORDS · *Lawrence Dewyatt Abrams* · 144
". . . I've learned to keep my marching boots shined, to love my man fiercely, to lock arms with my brothers forming safe houses, and to preserve my sanity by keeping my pencil sharpened."

BROTHER TO BROTHER: WORDS FROM THE HEART ·
Joseph F. Beam · 42
"I am most often rendered invisible, perceived as a threat to the family, or I am tolerated if I am silent and inconspicuous. I cannot go home as who I am, and that hurts deeply."

MENTORING GAY YOUTH · *Thom Bean* · 49
"Mentoring can be a two-edged sword. If the mentor or the protégé is not careful, mentoring can turn into a hustle, danger, or even death."

BECOMING A MOVEMENT · *Rodney Christopher* · 155
"Despite the contribution that African-Americans and Latinos made to starting the gay rights movement, that movement did not make much of an effort to respond to the problems and needs of gays and lesbians of color."

FEAR OF A GAY IDENTITY: A PERSONAL ACCOUNT ON INTERN-ALIZING HETEROSEXISM · *Geoffrey Giddings* · 17

"My family's attitude about homosexuality does not stray far from what is generally viewed as typical Caribbean heterosexism. When I think of coming out to my family, I do not fear persecution. What I am truly afraid of is the incredible disappointment and shame family members would feel knowing there is an 'antiman' in the family."

THOUGHTS ON TRADE/ENDING AN OBSESSION · *Edwin L. Greene* · 35

"Gay men who chase after trade are running after a discredited idea. Discredited because most gay men who have this obsession have suffered the physical, verbal, and emotional violence that comes with the territory. They're not even being sexually satisfied in the bargain."

WHY I'M NOT MARCHING · *David Frechette* · 131

"Mention gay racism to most white gays and their eyes roll toward Heaven as they attempt to stifle yawns."

I PAY THE BLACK TAX · *Mark Haile* · 124

"The Black Tax is having to assuage someone for the hundredth time, 'I'm harmless, really I am. I'm not doing Angry Negro today.' The Black Tax is the churning in my stomach that comes because I supposedly have the omnipotent ability to instill fear in others."

THE TRUTH ABOUT STONEWALL · *Mark Haile* · 164

". . . the Stonewall legend does concern people of color. If that sultry weekend's street theatre is to be regarded as the launching pad of the modern gay rights movement, then it is essential for us to know the key players who started it all: drag queens, hustlers, jailbait juveniles, and gay men and lesbians of color. The outcasts of gay life thus showed homosexual America how to make a fist, fight back, and win self-respect."

BEHIND THESE PRISON WALLS · *Eugene Harris* · 63
"As a black man confined to the crude world of incarceration, it has inspired me to take advantage of the opportunity to earn my GED and to read voraciously."

I AM A HOMOSEXUAL · *Essex Hemphill* · 150
"I have not chosen to isolate myself from my friends and community. There are valid reasons for doing so, but I feel that would contribute to the absence of visible, positive homosexual images—particularly images for the young, who must still discover their sexual identities awkwardly, dangerously, or sadly."

STAYING HEALTHY IN THE AGE OF AIDS · *Arnold Jackson* · 107
"Despite what you might think, those in power, those who are calling the shots in the war against AIDS do not want to see an end to this disease. AIDS is a multibillion-dollar-a-year industry."

THE LETTER · *Donald Keith Jackson* · 83
"Many letters and cards have been exchanged between us. Today I felt a strong need to pull out the first letter you sent to me telling me of your arrival in Beirut. You said that this is not a place to spend a vacation! It's the kind of place that could drive you to extreme boredom."

LOOKING FOR LOVE · *Jalal* · 88
"Very few of the men I had sex with held me or kissed me. These older men I was attracted to treated me like an object. Having sex with men who rarely showed me affection made me realize I needed more."

CLOSETS · *G. Winston James* · 67
"Nowadays, I frequent peep shows and have been to 'safer-sex clubs,' which are not unlike the pantry in my parents' first home. Little worlds that straight (and sometimes gay) men create to allow gay men to pretend to be free."

A PLACE AT THE ALTAR · *Lynwoodt Jenkins* · 147
"Tolerated *only* when measured by our octave range, athletic prowess, and/or our general public-pleasing abilities. Men, who, in the light of day, are looked upon in disdain, while in the cloaking darkness of night are desired, hunted, and insulted by dead presidents in exchange for illicit favors."

THE EMERGENCE OF AN AFRICAN GAY AND LESBIAN COMMUNITY · *Cary Alan Johnson* · 138
"Despite the allegations of African politicians that homosexuality is a purely Western phenomenon, most African nations have laws which prohibit sexual contact between men, statutes adopted mainly from the jurisprudence of the former colonial powers. The need for laws to regulate behaviors that do not exist has not yet been explained."

KISSING COUSIN · *R. Leigh (Tré) Johnson* · 72
"My mother and I moved in with my grandmother and the most beautiful black boy I had ever seen, my cousin Somba. It was love at first sight."

BENEATH THE VENEER · *Kheven L. LaGrone* · 13
"That white man smiled smugly at me. Was he confident enough to offer his leash to me, a black man and total stranger? Did he assume black men craved his leash? Perhaps he was baiting me, an anguished black man: 'Look niggah, I got one of your homeboys on a leash.'"

BREAKING SILENCE IN THE MIDDLE OF A HOLOCAUST · *Rodney McCoy, Jr.* · 97
"Writing this essay as an openly gay African-American health educator shatters the myth that gay and bisexual men don't exist in the black community. It also challenges the other myth that black gay and bisexual men do not serve as positive role models."

I HATE BASKETBALL · *Kevin McGruder* · 54
"I'm too shy and thin-skinned for the street game, which

is filled with banter and insults usually countered with displays of skill that silence the offender."

CONFRONTING ADVERSITY · *Bruce Morrow* · 128
"A good black man's hard to find because the ones out there are either gay or in jail! Isn't that the saying?"

DEAREST BROTHER SET · *Conrad R. Pegues* · 113
"I'm often deeply disturbed by the idea that I might lose you if you ever found out about me. It is easy for people to say, 'Well, you didn't need him anyway.' Deep down you know you need the love and support of other black men like you need water and air."

THE OTHER ORPHANS · *Robert E. Penn* · 101
"I wonder how my mother will handle it if I die before her. I wonder how my sister will take it."

LIKE THE WHITE GIRLS · *Tod A. Roulette* · 78
"We went to a black church, the only time I was around other black males my age. I admired them. They were cool like my father, so together and in-the-know. But they lived and breathed young, black, urban culture, and I instantly felt shut out."

COLORING OUTSIDE THE LINES:
AN ESSAY AT DEFINITION · *Reginald Shepherd* · 24
"When I realized or decided I was gay, somewhere around the sixth or seventh grade, that seemed another way of getting out, of getting somewhere *else*. (For me, sexual identity was a mode of social mobility.)"

DREADLOCKS · *Mark Simmons* · 9
"I remember an interviewer's remark that dreadlocks and suits didn't go together. 'It's because it's a concept that you had never thought of,' I wanted to say, but I smiled and counted the seconds until I would be ushered out to the elevators."

GIL'S STORY · *Sur Rodney (Sur)* · 57

"Soon after his return to Paris, Gil once again fell in love. This one, unlike the others, was special. He knew it with all his heart. Their lovemaking was different and so was his special talent. Jean-Marc was a skater, one of the rare special dancers on ice whose talents he believed could be trained to perfection."

PROJECT ERASURE · *Fabian Thomas* · 134

". . . I think of how we, as lesbians and gay men, participate in our erasure. We keep ourselves separate, attack one another, negate one another's existence, and shorten our own lives."

FIGHTING WORDS

INTRODUCTION:
A MULTIPLICITY OF WITNESS

"Black gay men have the difficult terrain of being black in racist society, gay in homophobic society, and gay in the black community."

—THOMAS GLAVE, AUTHOR[1]

"The black man in our culture represents so many archetypes—some of them scary, some of them powerful, some of them primitive."

—JOHN BARTLETT, MEN'S WEAR DESIGNER[2]

"To be black and male in the United States is not only to live complexities of another's making but also to attempt to construct a self and chart a life, however difficult, of one's own."

—CHARLES H. ROWELL, PROFESSOR OF ENGLISH/EDITOR[3]

When the African-American painter Beauford Delaney (who would later become James Baldwin's mentor and friend) was a young art student in New York City, "His shyness," writes his biographer, "made the model-painter relationship difficult."[4] And since the model would be completely nude, it was a great relief to Delaney "to discover the unwritten rule that black painters not attend life classes when the female models were white."[5] The fact that he was a black *gay* man didn't matter to the art school administrators. All that mattered was that he was a *black* man, a potential threat to white women. The absurdness of this rule, based purely on race prejudice, is underscored by this notion: "A black gay man is an oxymoron, according to our cultural constructions," states Thomas Glave, an award-winning black gay writer, "because how can you be a rapist and a sissy at the same time?"[6]

Throughout American history, black male sexuality has been a thing to fear as well as a thing of curiosity and myth. That mixture of fear and mythology is what caused white Southern lynch mobs to castrate their black victims and take the severed penises home as souvenirs.

Even today, the image of the black superstud "has been absorbed into white gay culture through the gay press and especially in gay pornography. The myth of the black stud as the ideal sex partner is even present in the culture of gay Harlem."[7] A private sex club called Blatino, for example, is a byproduct of this mythology. They shamelessly exclude any black or Latino gay man who does not fit this superstud image. The root of this myth dates to the slave auction block where the physical condition of the slaves determined who was bought or sold. This included the careful inspection of the male genitalia, to ensure the creation of slave progeny.

Then, as now, black men were regarded as brutal, aggressive, sexually uninhibited, primitive, intellectually immature. This scary but titillating image is what brought many pleasure-seeking whites to Harlem in the 1920s, during that period known as the Harlem Renaissance. Because of its "sexually tolerant population," writes the historian Eric Garber, "and its quasi-legal nightlife,, Harlem offered an oasis to white homosexuals."[8]

"In the homosexual iconography of the period," writes Steven Watson, another historian, "the black male vied with the swarthy Italian youth and the sailor in uniform as the iconic love object."[9]

The black male in general, and the black gay male in particular, continues to be seen as exotic, as the other, as someone to be desired sexually, but not to be taken seriously on an intellectual level. The black gay man, especially, is someone "not important to be discussed at large."[10] Whenever he appears in mainstream white society or white gay society, his presence causes him "to be followed on the street, treated rudely, ignored, or barred from certain premises."[11] "That's what defines me," laments a Harlem gay man. "My color. Even though I choose to be gay, a gay black man, it's my color that decides where I go, who I can go with, or what I can do. . . ."[12]

Within the black community, where many black gay men prefer to live, "homosexuality is still a no-no, an unmentionable topic in most households and churches."[13]

Because of its unspeakableness, "too many of us spend our lives in the closet," writes the novelist James Earl Hardy. "And one of the best ways to do that is to adopt the B-boy[14] stance. And B-boys with the indirect support of the community, fool themselves into thinking that, because they are so hard, because no one knows and probably won't figure them out, they can't be homosexual."[15]

They may "throw their masculinity around for the entire world"[16] to take notice of, but this "exaggerated take on manhood"[17] is really an act of desperation. They've "swallowed whole the phony and perverse John Wayne definition of manhood," writes the author Earl Ofari Hutchinson, "that real men talked and acted tough, shed no tears, and never showed their emotions."[18] They have regarded homosexuality as "a kinky contrivance of white males and females that reflected the decadence of white America."[19] Ironically, at the same time they proudly walk the streets of black America wearing clothes emblazoned with the logo of the late Perry Ellis—a white gay man—and sing love songs in falsetto, a vocal style that is "part of the history of effeminacy"[20] and "has the clearest links to homosexuality."[21]

In the absence of true role models and male rites of passage ceremonies, these young men compensate through bravado, braggadoccio, and often violence. Like all humans, these young men, like their older counterparts, need love, kindness, concern, respect, guidance, and a helping hand.

That is why this anthology of essays exists. And why it is called *Fighting Words*. Its goal is to use words, language, as a weapon against despair, self-loathing, and loneliness. Many black gay men are making a valiant attempt through the written word to reach out to other black gay men and help them to heal the wounds inflicted on them by a racist, homophobic society. "We have the most potential to shatter the prevailing stereotypes," states Thomas Glave, in a newspaper interview. "We have a chance to be ourselves, invent something new."[22]

In the thirty essays, the writers share common concerns—self-identity, self-acceptance, self-esteem, black gay brotherhood and camaraderie, heterosexist (black and white) oppression, and white (gay and straight) racism.

Through its "multiplicity of witnesses,"[23] "we're trying to make sense of ourselves to ourselves."[24]

It is my fervent hope that *Fighting Words* will be a stepping-stone toward serious self-examination, self-knowledge, and self-healing for each and every black gay man who decides to read it and embrace it. I also hope it will persuade straight black men that "they should be the last ones on the planet to jettison other blacks who may be in a position to make valuable contributions to the struggle for political and economic empowerment."[25]

—Charles Michael Smith
New York, New York
October 1998

NOTES

1. Viet Dinh, "My Little Secret, Thomas Glave Wins an O. Henry Award," *New York Blade News*, 24 Oct. 1997, p. 33.

2. David Colman, "Big Muscles, Big Attitude: Fashion's Ideal Man," *The New York Times*, 4 Aug. 1996, p. 46.

3. Charles H. Rowell, "Signing Yourself: An Afterword," *Shade: An Anthology of Fiction by Gay Men of African Descent*, edited by Bruce Morrow and Charles H. Rowell (New York: Avon Books, 1996), p. 341.

4. David Leeming, *Amazing Grace: A Life of Beauford Delaney* (New York: Oxford University Press, 1998), p. 68.

5. Ibid., p. 68.

6. Dinh, "My Little Secret," p. 33.

7. William G. Hawkeswood, *One of the Children: Gay Black Men in Harlem* (Berkeley: University of California Press, 1996), edited by Alex W. Costley, pp. 157–158.

8. Eric Garber, "A Spectacle in Color: The Lesbian and Gay Subculture of Jazz Age Harlem," in *Hidden from History: Reclaiming the Gay & Lesbian Past,* edited by Martin Bauml Duberman, Martha Vicinus, and George Chauncey, Jr. (New York: New American Library, 1989), p. 329 (paperback).

9. Steven Watson, *The Harlem Renaissance: Hub of African-American Culture, 1920–1930* (New York: Pantheon, 1995), p. 134.

10. Dinh, "My Little Secret," p. 33.

11. Hawkeswood, *One of the Children,* p. 157.

12. Ibid., p. 99.

13. James Earl Hardy, *B-Boy Blues* (Boston: Alyson Publications, 1994), p. 28.

14. Ibid., p. 25. "They are the boyz who stand on street corners, doin' their own vogue— striking that 'cool pose' against a pole, a storefront, up against or on a car. . . . They style and profile in their baggy jeans or pants falling somewhere between their waists and knees, barely holding onto their behinds, their undergear pulled up over their waists. They kick the pavement in sidewalk-stompin' boots and low- and high-top, high-priced sneakers, oftentimes worn loose, unlaced, open, with their trousers tucked inside."

15. Ibid., p. 28.

16. Ibid., p. 27.

17. Ibid., p. 27.

18. Earl Ofari Hutchinson, Ph.D., *The Crisis in Black and Black* (Los Angeles: Middle Passage Press, 1998), p. 93.

19. Ibid., p. 94.

20. Wayne Koestenbaum, *The Queen's Throat: Opera, Homosexuality, and the Mystery of Desire* (New York: Poseidon Press, 1993), p. 164.

21. Ibid., p. 165.

22. Dinh, "My Little Secret," p. 33.

23. This wonderful term was used by the novelist E. L. Doctorow in an interview on a New York City radio station to describe reality as seen through the eyes of several people.

24. Terry McMillan, editor, *Breaking Ice: An Anthology of Contemporary African-American Fiction* (New York: Penguin Books, 1990), p. xxi (paperback).

25. Hutchinson, *The Crisis in Black and Black,* p. 99.

· I ·

IDENTITY

DREADLOCKS

by Mark Simmons

After almost a year of sending out résumés wrapped in twenty-nine-cent wrappers, job interviews that lasted less than sixty seconds, two-day temp jobs, and unemployment checks twice a month, I stared at myself in a mirror, my dreadlocks beginning to touch my shoulders, and picked them up, one by one, until they covered the bottom of the sink, shorn. I knew that the rejection that slid off my skin like sweat was, in part, because of my hairstyle. With it a college degree carried absolutely no credibility. That same lack of credibility would be faced with a look of "I don't believe you." Through this experience I had learned that load after load of racism, letter-shaped gravel, is still being dumped, steadily and without hesitation, upon African Americans, hitting our heads and shoulders like the weight of wet concrete. Dreadlocks, for me, provided an armor of self-love and pride that steeled my thoughts, where the racism ran like water onto the ground.

Cutting my dreadlocks combined with an "it's-who-you-know" advantage propelled me into the realm of a Hollywood dream factory. I agreed to work as a six-dollar-an-hour page at a major Hollywood studio. I was in. For six months, interviews led me to this unexpected chance. During that time, I had calculated that I probably had sent more than one hundred résumés and handwritten applications to this studio's human resources department. They sent me a letter informing me that they kept résumés and applications on file for six months.

One afternoon, full of brazen self-confidence, I planted myself into their reception area for an hour before they politely asked me to leave. From a friend I learned about frequent openings in the mailroom. I found out who was the manager and gave him my résumé. I bugged him a bit every so often until he told me to go deliver my résumé to the Guest Relations Department. A couple of weeks later, I got a call for an interview, after which I was hired with twenty other applicants. Looking back, as I directed a studio tour group into a soundstage, watched them pull down their sunglasses and peer at the expansive space, I concluded that I never would have gotten this job with a head full of dreadlocks. This is the place where stereotypes are manufactured like candy. Enough racism to fit into your mouth, formed in bite-sized pieces.

Once half a year of indentured servitude was completed, the opportunity to find other employment on the lot was encouraged. Surely if I had cut my hair early on, the numerous interviews that I bounced from like a restless basketball would have garnered a position in the homogenizing advertising field.

Throughout the two-week training period, former pages were paraded before us like royalty. Their success stories, blowing around the lot, symbolized tumbleweeds of opportunities we had the chance to seize. Yet, for me, as an African-American gay man, I would be afforded these same chances, for three times the amount of work as a white person. This department interviewed more than fifty people for twenty part-time jobs. At the initial interview process I counted to see how many African Americans were at the audition/job interview. There were three of us. Surprisingly, we were all hired. At the end of our training, we shared brunch at my house in the Silverlake district of Los Angeles. Inevitably, talk centered on the reality of few hours at ridiculously low wages.

Dreadlocks, when I wore them, afforded me the luxury of being very ethnic without doing anything. African Americans—on the streets, in the restaurants—always gave me looks that said, Go, brother. Wearing dreadlocks made me feel like a New York boho, even though I was an Arkansan by birth. I felt special when I received the attention of strangers, both brothers and sisters, who would touch the locks, their fingers holding the hair I'd grown, coarsened, and kinked by the ritual twisting.

By the time my dreadlocks, hanging in neat rows, had grown past my ears, it would take me almost an hour to "do" them. After washing them, which I did three times a week, I would put a dollop of Vaseline in the center of my palm and coat my dreads to help retain the moisture of the water. Dreadlocks are very easy to dry out and Vaseline acts as a shield. For me, this was the true drag of wearing dreadlocks. Of course, you could go without washing them for a while, but they tend to get matted less attractively. Even though my dreadlocks were pristinely neat and clean, they still did not go over well at the time of my unemployment. I remember an interviewer's remark that dreadlocks and suits didn't go together. "It's because it's a concept that you had never thought of," I wanted to say, but I smiled and counted the seconds until I would be ushered out to the elevators.

After bouncing around the job market in Los Angeles at numerous advertising and public relations agencies, I still lacked the qualities of "fitting in." In fact, one of the reasons I left my last job was primarily because they felt dreadlocks conveyed the wrong impression. Yet the idea of a multicultural American twentysomething ideal vision clouded my eyes and ears. Almost an endless supply of weekly interviews, gleaned from my answering machine, began with raised eyebrows and befuddled expressions. Instinctively, I knew that it was my appearance, not my skills or qualifications. That realization hit me like the last punch before a fighter is knocked out. "So that's it," I said to myself one day as I drove on the Hollywood 101 Freeway. White folks are scared of brothers in dreadlocks. This fear stems from the fact that by wearing dreadlocks we are embracing our entire culture, slave history included, in a subtle, yet celebratory manner. As black leather jackets and Afros epitomized the fiery Black Panther Party segment of the civil rights movement, dreadlocks and kufis symbolize the 1990s version of recognizing our history and building from there.

Wearing dreadlocks gave me a sense of freedom, of self, primarily, that remains elusive in their absence. I loved my dreadlocks. I loved the way the wind teased them as I drove my car on the clogged streets. I loved them as I stared at their shadow outlined on the paper I read outside my house in Silverlake, the grass crushed under my weight. I loved inspecting the imprints, left the night before, on my face in the bathroom mirror the next morning. I loved the way they smelled after I bathed them in apple mint shampoo. I loved the ten-second conversations held at intersections with African-American women driving Rabbit convertibles asking me where I had my hair done. I loved the way people managed to say "Hello," especially in L.A., silently mouthed. I loved the way they tore through the air as I danced at a disco, strobe lights illuminating them for milliseconds. And I loved the way they felt as they wiped the sweat from my face as I worked out at the gym. I loved them because they made me feel more accepted in American culture than I've felt at any other time. Only four years out of twenty-eight years can be a long time to be able to feel something that is our race's undeniable rights.

Homogenized to fit into the mainstream, conservative dominant society, I walk my journey and view life through the eyes of an African-American gay man. Dreadlocks gave me the pride, unleashed, that I carry with me every day. And, yes, it's my duty to make sure it's noticed daily.

As I led the group through the door at the end of the two-hour tour, I waited until a brother with dreadlocks passed. "Wait a second, brother," I said to him. "I like your dreadlocks." "Thanks, man," he replied, his glistening teeth catching sunlight that drenched his honey-colored face. I nervously pulled my wallet out and said, "Look." Just one reminder of my time with dreadlocks, stamped on a California driver's license. "That's cool, brother," he said, taking off his sunglasses, his eyes much more animated than before. "Why'd you cut them?" I smiled, and told him it would take another two hours. "Keep them as long as you can," I advised.

BENEATH THE VENEER

by Kheven L. LaGrone

"When you control a man's thinking you do not have
to worry about his actions. You do not have to tell him
not to stand here or go yonder. He will find his 'proper
place' and will stay in it. You do not need to send him
to the back door. He will go without being told. In fact,
if there is no back door, he will cut one for his special
benefit."

—CARTER G. WOODSON[1]

"Any colored man gains unquestioned admission into
innumerable places the moment he appears as the me-
nial attendant of some white person, where he could
not cross the threshold in his own right as a well-
dressed and well-behaved master of himself."

—GEORGE W. CABLE IN 1895[2]

"Is that black man wearing a leash?" I asked a friend at a
party in San Francisco, the "gay mecca." The host was a white
artist showcasing his portraits of black men. Almost all the
guests were black.

"That's right," answered my friend, verifying what I thought
I saw. "The white man's the master, the black man's his slave."
I looked in anguish as this average-looking white man strutted
in, surveyed the room commandingly, flaunted his beautiful

13

black buck. So shocked by this symbol of defeated black mas-culinity, I forgot which politically correct mask to hide behind. Seeking solace, I turned to the brothers sitting next to me.

"But that's just the S and M scene . . . this is the Castro," one offered.

"I think it's beautiful, it took a lot of guts to be who he is," rationalized another—defending the black "slave."

"Freedom of expression . . . freedom of choice," one argued.

I looked up to see the white man grinning smugly at me. The black man fetched him a plate of food.

That night, I felt hurt, anger, and disgust for black men. Since that party, I have read a personal ad by a black man asking, "Are you white man enough to ride this plantation?" Another self-defined "colored boy" sought "natural white male domination." At San Francisco's notorious Dore Street Fair, a black man danced with a Confederate flag hanging from his back pocket and a huge penis bulging from his ripped jeans.

I told three white gay liberals about the black man on the leash; they argued that "It was just a fantasy." One even added, "It's just a personal taste—like preferring strawberry ice cream over rainbow sherbet." Appalled, I wondered how many white men had ever smiled at me with a taste for leash-ing me.

The black man on a leash was allegorical. If a black man was to be accepted into the "gay mecca," he must wear his leash: a white lover "proved" he was not "bitter and angry"; affected speech and feigned hair tosses "showed" he was not "too black." Black men themselves "bragged" about "being exposed to white people" and "knowing how to act 'round white folks"—sounding like wild black beasts "bragging" about being successfully raised and trained in captivity. So at the party, the Great White Hunter paraded his captured black beast—his noble savage, wild African savage, spear-chucker, spook, ape, porch monkey, jigaboo, playful primitive, spade, nigra, brute, jungle bunny, buck, coon, or nigger. For that black man wearing the leash, did reality follow fantasy or did fan-tasy follow reality?

That white man smiled smugly at me. Was he confident

enough to offer his leash to me, a black man and total stranger? Did he assume black men craved his leash? Perhaps he was baiting me, an anguished black man: "Look, niggah, I got one of your homeboys on a leash."

How should I have reacted? Should I have shrugged my shoulders; should I have giggled and feigned a hair toss so not to be branded "too militant" or "too angry and bitter"?

How many white men have accused me of being a black racist, or have accused me of exhibiting "that (angry black) attitude," when they were really accusing me of not being their nigger-on-a-leash?

White supremacy greatly influenced American history and culture; yet too few white men openly admit harboring white supremacist notions. Most choose to believe that such notions are the domain of a few ignorant individuals. Many white gay men have argued that their own *re*pression has enlightened them and made them more sensitive to the *op*pression of black men. Ironically, these same white men often eroticized their white supremacist images of the beastly black male. Their claim: "It's just a fantasy."

The white gay media often reflected this white supremacist attitude. More than one white gay publication listed "black men" as a sexual fetish. Other fetishes listed included feet, bondage, dildoes, and homoerotic suicide. I never saw white men listed as a fetish.

But sadly, black men were often the most staunch and callous white supremacists. In the "gay mecca," black men sneered invectives like "nigger-ish" and "ghetto girl" at each other. Black men "bragged" that they did not date black men. Black men described very handsome white men as "Nordic Gods." It was fashionable for black men in the "gay mecca" to say, "I don't see color, I see people"; but it was more common for black men to avert their eyes when passing other black men on the street.

Their white supremacy was their business. I could have ignored these black men; but I believe we black men ignore, deny too much already.

I opened this essay with a quotation from the black historian

Carter G. Woodson. I wonder if these black men had ever read it before. Who controlled their thinking? I listened to black men "brag" that their sleeping with white men breaks racial barriers by "proving" to white men that they are human. I listened to a black man make an excuse for the many, many white men who slept with him only to see if black men really are animals in bed. He was hurt that the white men never called him again.

A black man regularly complained about white men being "racist" dogs and pigs, but he continued to sleep with them. I listened to a black poet read a piece in which he complained about his many white sex partners' "Gorilla Fantasy." Who held these black men's leashes? They complained, but stayed in their "proper place."

I too have the right to wear leashes; someone called it freedom of choice. But if I CHOOSE to perch white men on pedestals, then I place them in a position where they must look down to see me. If I CHOOSE to deify whiteness, then I have no right to be angry when a white man shows human frailties. If I CHOOSE to glorify white skin, I cannot blame white men for MY self-hatred.

NOTES

1. Carter G. Woodson, *The Mis-Education of the Negro* (Lawrenceville, N.J.: Africa World Press).

2. Taken from Lawrence J. Friedman, *White Savage* (Englewood Cliffs, N.J.: Prentice-Hall, 1970). Original quotation taken from *The Silent South Together with the Freedman's Case in Equity and the Convict Lease System* (New York: Charles Scribner's Sons, 1895), pp. 21–22.

Fear of a Gay Identity: A Personal Account on Internalizing Heterosexism

by Geoffrey Giddings

". . . where is my reflection? I am most often rendered
invisible, perceived as a threat to the family, or am tolerated if I am silent and inconspicuous. I cannot go home
as who I am and that hurts me deeply."

—JOSEPH BEAM, *In the Life*[1]

My recent coming out to some friends and family members
has caused me to think seriously about an important issue in
my life and, I suspect, an issue that most homosexual men and
women confront every day. Why is it so often painful to come
out to straight people, even those who profess love for us. For
me, dealing with this issue has taken a few years of fierce
internal struggle before landing me at a place where my soul,
mind, and conscience rest somewhat peacefully.

The first revelation of my sexuality to a straight person was
my female best friend, Angela. I had been out of college one
year and was about to begin teaching. Encouraged by a friend
who was a tremendous source of inspiration, I felt that I should
be more honest about my life to people I cared about. And, of
course, close friends served as a good warm-up before I would
let my family in on the big secret.

I was petrified to reveal my deepest, darkest secret, even to
one of my best friends. I was certain that Angela would be
repulsed and would want to end our friendship. I actually
looked forward to this reaction as an easy way out of the

shame I imagined I would feel when discussing my sexuality with straight people. To my surprise she was open and understanding. She said she had suspected I was gay and that she had been afraid I would be offended if she asked. She was right; I would have been offended because I believed being thought of as gay meant I was being considered less than whole. I even felt ashamed that she had suspected me of being gay. I thought, Gee, what did I do to give myself away?

Angela's acceptance was no relief to me. Her acceptance meant that now I would have to deal with her knowing my secret. I thought this might mean she would always have thoughts of my being some sort of freak. Feelings of fear, guilt, and shame would always surface when hopeful but dejected female suitors asked if I were gay or when family members would pointedly inquire as to why I didn't have a girlfriend. So before coming out to other close friends and family members, I had to find some way of feeling more comfortable with my homosexuality.

After much thought, I began to realize that this confusion resulted from internalized heterosexism. Coming out to straight friends and family members was forcing me to reflect on a heated tension flaming within me, a tension ignited by the belief among many people of African descent that African and homosexual identities do not rightly coexist. It was only after my good friend nurtured my gay pride by introducing me to the works of Essex Hemphill and Joseph Beam that I worked up enough courage to reveal my sexuality to my two male college buddies after graduation. But the fact that I was not even in the same region of the country as they were helped me deal with the fear that they might lose respect for me, despite their outward acceptance.

As a child my psyche had taken quite a beating. I received much teasing from my peers because of an early childhood skin disease. I held what I now view as a strange reverence for white cultural aesthetics and was attracted to only the lightest-skinned members of my community. The first attraction I had for a man was a light-skinned friend of my older brother. This preference for whiteness during early childhood years is fairly common among black children who are not taught to love themselves. In class I hear my students call their dark-skinned classmates "black" with utter disgust in their voices. This phenomenon is just one manifestation of European cultural hegemony upon people of African descent.

I came to the States in 1980. My self-esteem was slowly strengthening as I began to excel academically. But strangely enough, this is the time I became aware that I was emotionally and sexually attracted to males. Throughout secondary school I secretly fantasized about males but did not have the confidence nor the encouragement to partake of the forbidden fruit. That didn't happen until well into my college career.

Five years at a predominantly white university forced me to seek self-affirmation from the few sisters and brothers on campus. It was in college that I learned just how intractable racism is in our society. In fact, my growing interest in my heritage inspired me to major in African and African-American history. The small nucleus of support made me comfortable. We all learned that knowledge is the key to overcoming the white cultural hegemony that made us unhappy on, and sometimes off, campus. Although I was well aware of my sexuality at this point, I believed nobody would understand, not even the openly gay folks, who were mostly white.

I refused to seek support from the white gay organization on campus. Despite the fact that this gay and lesbian organization was very popular and accepted by the entire campus community, I felt that whites could not help any African-American dealing with race issues, and certainly not a person of African descent who is struggling against the unique heterosexism found in the African/Caribbean-American communities.

So I locked myself up in the campus's microcosmic African-American community. It was there that I sought affirmation as a man of African descent to heal the scars I suffered when I was much younger. I realized I needed to build my self-esteem and what better way of doing that than by becoming proud of my African roots. This idea of acquiring positive self-esteem through knowledge of self and race pride is encouraged by such African-American social theorists as Dr. Jawanza Kunjufu and Dr. Molefi Kete Asante. By the end of my college years, I had come to see the benefits of this philosophy.

I became so in love with "blackness" that whenever I came down from school, family members teased me about always doing, reading, and talking about "black stuff." But when they finally realized my passion was not just a phase, the teasing stopped. I am proud that I have been able to encourage many people, including my older brothers, to seek out knowledge on the great legacy our forebears have left.

All this notwithstanding, I was becoming incredibly miserable. My self-esteem was not as strong as it should have been. I was too busy denying a very important part of myself.

Despite the fact that I was a socially well-adjusted person and still had no interest in dating girls, it was still assumed that I was straight simply because I was seen as a positive brother. I often took this assumption as a compliment because I had accepted the narrow definition of masculinity constructed by many in the African-American community. The result of this self-effacing compromise was that I encouraged heterosexism.

During my first year out of college, I attended a black men's support group sponsored by the Association of Black Psychologists, where the issue of homosexuality came up often. Each time it did, I simply shriveled up like a coward. I wanted to share my experience with those brothers because my story would have provided a unique perspective to them, most of whom did not believe they knew any gay person. But I feared that all the respect they had for me would have been thrown right out the door. Perhaps not, but I felt it was too risky. Thus, disassociation from my sexual reality was the price I paid to seek out and celebrate the riches of my heritage and to commune peacefully with my brothers and sisters.

In addition to my African ancestry, I am very proud of my Caribbean heritage. My chest swells when I think of my membership in a tradition that has produced the likes of Marcus Garvey, C.L.R. James, Walter Rodney, Kwame Toure, Michael Manley, Shirley Chisholm, and Derek Walcott. Living in Crown Heights in Brooklyn, New York, I was enveloped by Caribbean people: our styles, our languages, our beauty. However, what troubles me about this community is its pernicious heterosexism. This attitude of social intolerance and religion influencing fear and hate of homosexuality is well-documented. My family's attitude about homosexuality does not stray far from what is generally viewed as typical Caribbean hetero-sexism. When I think of coming out to my family I do not fear persecution. What I am truly afraid of is the incredible disappointment and shame family members would feel know-ing there is an "antiman" in the family. As much as they love me, my family would detest being held accountable by neighbors and friends for having reared someone who vio-lates their social and sexual tradition. What I also fear is the intense shame of homosexuality that even I myself have inter-nalized after years of being told that it is something unclean and sinful.

Growing up in Guyana, I remember there was a flamboy-ant man whom we called Antiman Desmond, who would parade in fabulous costumes and dance in the Mashramani Independence Day carnivals. In retrospect, I find it strange but not surprising that as a child I never fathomed this man having a real life. I thought of him as just a jester, and that is what most people around me encouraged. I will admit, however, that part of me always admired this man, who seemed free to live as he wanted to. Nonetheless, the fact that Antiman Desmond was shunned by the community, sent a clear message to me that homosexuality is not a viable way to live. This is the sort of limited view of homosexuality that I felt I was up against whenever I considered coming out to my family.

As I continued to conceal my sexuality, a question that increasingly haunted me was how is it that a man with such strong race pride should suffer ambiguous feelings concern-ing his own sexuality. Asante and others had instilled a be-lief that when one is proud of one's heritage, one is almost emotionally unbeatable. But as I thought of how I viewed my sexuality, I realized that there was something lacking in this formula when applied to my feelings about myself as a homosexual man. I could stand tall and firmly announce my pride in being of African and Caribbean descent, but my head was cast down whenever I admitted my homosexual-ity, even to myself. I began to be very critical of these insecure feelings of shame and fear. I started to see that my sexuality is very much an intrinsic part of who I am, and that the effects of heterosexism in our society can be personally as crippling as that of racism.

As Essex Hemphill said, "If I had read a book like *In the Life* when I was sixteen, there might have been one less mask for me to put aside later in life."[2] Growing up, whether gay or straight, we are all naturally affirmed as heterosexuals by this society. Because of this fact, I believe that we older and more conscious homosexual men and women should take on the duty to do whatever is within our power to combat the damaging images of homosexuality this society perpetuates by affirming the natural sexuality of young people who are aware of their homosexuality. This is simply in sync with our long tradition of elders "looking after" the youth.

Accessibility to a network of gay role models among friends and associates is crucial to gay men and women in developing a positive self-identity. I have been fortunate to have developed a best friend and other good friends who are in the life. It is this sort of support I wish I had had earlier to affirm a self-image that is only now recovering from heterosexist abuse.

Now, some might wonder why come out at all. Why put oneself through the emotional fatigue and run the risk of being ostracized by friends and family. Well, the problem is, I want to send a clear message to all people I love that I would appreciate them loving me for the whole of who I am.

It is detrimental to my psychological well-being to be halted by feelings of shame and guilt whenever I think of simply being honest with my family about who I am. Sisters and brothers who fear the ramifications of coming out should be assured that there is support, strength, and salvation in numbers, unity, and consciousness. But ultimate responsibility for change lies with our larger community whose oppressive intolerance often forces us, especially our youth, to contemplate suicide. It is our duty as gay folks to help carry the torch to light America's path to becoming a truly just society. But before we take up the torch, many of us, myself included, need to be girded with the belief that our sexuality is a legitimate and beautiful reality, instead of something sinful and repulsive.

NOTES

1. Joseph Beam, *In the Life* (Los Angeles: Alyson Publications, 1986), p. 231.

2. Essex Hemphill, *Brother to Brother* (Los Angeles: Alyson Publications, 1991), p. xv.

COLORING OUTSIDE THE LINES:
AN ESSAY AT DEFINITION

─────────────

by *Reginald Shepherd*

For Chris Cutrone, who has helped me work through these conundrums, both intellectually and emotionally.

This is a story I tell myself about who I am, a story that, in the nature of all telling, conceals as much as it reveals. Like the Muses in the Greek poet Hesiod's *Theogony*, it can make lies seem true, but it can also tell the truth. That story has constituted who I am, exactly by means of the reductions, simplifications, and exclusions that make it a narrative. As Oscar Wilde wrote many years ago, the one duty we owe to history is to rewrite it.

While split subjectivity and alienation—social, psychic, somatic—are not the most pressingly material problems facing black people in late twentieth-century America (they might be the substance of racism—as a reading of the Martinican psychoanalyst and theorist of colonized psychology Frantz Fanon's *Black Skin, White Masks* will confirm—but they're not the sum of the experience of black people, even "as" black people), they have been central to my not-as-unique-as-I'd-like-to-imagine life. I'm told that, in our perennially if not terminally postmodern condition, psychic displacement is neither unusual nor lamentable, but I've never found much comfort in the vertiginous consolations of theory. Having always lacked and longed for a stabilized identity, I'm not ready to celebrate its always already having been decentered. The French psychoanalytic theorist Jacques Lacan, of course, has pointed out that identity is itself a lack, or the compensation for a lack: It is exactly the longing to "be someone" that needs to be questioned. Who would that be, exactly, and why? And, always, who's asking?

This is a story about constructing an identity outside the identity, constituting an identity in isolation. It's a story the French Symbolist poet Arthur Rimbaud wrote over a hundred years ago, with the most exquisite concision: *"Je est un autre"*: "I is an other." Indeed, in both thought and deed. Consider this essay a gloss on that line.

Mine is a deracinated existence both psychically and socially, in which the "blackness" with which I grapple is largely abstract. My identity has largely formed itself (sometimes through "my" own initiative, sometimes despite me) through negations and refusals: most especially of myself, insofar as that self is defined as "black." For me, to be black and to be gay have been two radically discrete subject positions, which to a large extent have contradicted each other, except to increase my sense of the lack of any position called *mine*, much less *me*. There has, of course, been no lack of positions, or should I write *places*, into which several varieties of others have wished to put me, but none have fit. Or, should I say, *I* have never fit.

When I was growing up in the Bronx, poor, isolated, and, as far as everyone except my mother was concerned (and even she sometimes had her doubts), too smart for my own good, "black" was something I didn't particularly want to be. My desire not to be black was coterminous with, though not identical to, my desire not to be oppressed. Everyone around me in the projects was black; everyone was poor. It seemed there must be some essential connection between blackness and deprivation. (I didn't realize until much later that "blackness" itself is the product of privation.) Being smart in school, an "egghead," a "teacher's pet," wasn't appreciated at all, certainly not by the kids who used to sit on my stomach at recess and bang my head into the playground pavement for their amusement and my edification. But being smart was my way of getting a scholarship to private school, my ticket to another world. In private school there were very few black students, none of them poor; there was, however, a separate black PTA. Being smart was my way out of the Bronx, and it worked. Being smart was also my way out of being black, which "worked" much more ambiguously.

In private school I wasn't particularly well liked, partly because I was neither docile nor well behaved, and partly because there was something inherently unlikable about a nappy-headed black boy from the ghetto who got better grades than all those white children whose parents were paying a *lot* of money to the Riverdale Country Day School. I was marked by my very presence as someone who didn't know his place; I was reminded of that place often. As the headmaster kindly informed me, I was there only on sufferance. *Sufferance*, I thought. *What a beautiful word*. And now I get to use it in a sentence of my own. "Problem" or not, I was acknowledged to be *different*, not like all those *other* black people, the ones not special enough to be granted such a generous dispensation. "He's very difficult—*but so bright*." To be different was all I wanted out of life, to be an *individual, unique*, not like those people I kept getting mistaken for because of the color of my skin. Frantz Fanon wrote some time ago of the colonial invitation to identity-through-loss-of-identity, the operation by which to be different from those who are different makes you (almost) the same, as long as you don't look too hard. That was an invitation I eagerly accepted. After all, I *was* already at the party, wasn't I?

When I realized or decided I was gay, somewhere around the sixth or seventh grade, that seemed another way of getting out, of getting somewhere *else*. (For me, sexual identity was a mode of social mobility.) The things I felt and thought and quickly started reading everything I could about, in porno magazines and gay lib books and concerned cover stories in *Newsweek*, certainly had nothing to do with anything that went on at the corner of Crotona Avenue and East 183rd Street, nothing to do with black people or poverty. Sigmund Freud wrote somewhere that homosexuality is a way out, but I needed no prompting to start eagerly on my way. I'm speaking here not of my desire, which, however constructed, I remember experiencing as both fixed and constant, but of what I chose to make of that desire, the imaginary identifications and investments in which I engaged on that basis. I could certainly have been homosexual without becoming gay, without building a sense of self around my desire. Many men do, black, white, or otherwise; I've had sex with several of them, often in cars.

Being gay certainly seemed preferable to being black, however mediated the forms with which homosexuality presented itself to me. That mediated quality was part of gay identity's appeal. I never heard anybody in my neighborhood say anything bad about being gay. I never heard anybody say anything at all. Being gay didn't register as a possibility there, except for episodes of *Baretta* about boy prostitutes, and anything on TV was more glamourous than the life that had me. On the other hand, my mother constantly warned me that a nigger would just as soon stab you in the back as look at you, and don't you forget it. Those white people, they stuck together; those Puerto Ricans, they did too, especially when they were lying to cover up the beatings one always gave me. So did those Chinese, look how they had all those businesses and we had nothing, and we'd been here three hundred years. (Or was it four hundred?) But not those niggers. Us niggers. It seemed to me that maybe those gay people stuck together too. Even *Everything You Always Wanted to Know About Sex but Were Afraid to Ask* said that, as it avuncularly led its presumptively heterosexual reader through those sordid dens of homosexual maladjustment. So perhaps I could be one of those gays; perhaps they could be me.

For a white middle-class man, as central by birthright as can be, homosexuality is a displacement into a degree (and only into a degree) of marginality. But for a poor black boy from the Bronx projects (as neat a self-description as one could conjure up), occupying the opposite place or lack of place in the social spectrum (what I might call the subject position of subjection), homosexuality, conceived by people black and white alike as both a white and a middle-class phenomenon, can appear as an opportunity to displace displacement, to move toward the center. Gayness appears as a space outside of blackness, identity as utopia: my nowhere. To quote the poet

Wallace Stevens in a context he would find unrecognizable, all
sorts of favors fall from it.

Whatever my imaginary identifications, my gay life (such as
it has been) began at the onset of an extended leave from
college (Bennington, intermittently the most expensive college
in the nation: I've always been a scholarship boy). I moved
from Vermont to Boston, a city friends told me was a great
intellectual and cultural mecca. They were clearly being face-
tious. There I finally *met* gay men in numbers greater than two
or three. I had developed my vociferously held "gay identity"
in isolation, both longing for and apprehensive of others who
might be like me. Those others, as it happened, turned out *not*
to be like me. Most of the gay men I met were white (Boston
is hardly a haven of integration, social *or* psychic), and most
of them were just not as welcoming of their oppressed darker
brothers as I had been led to believe they would be by the gay
liberation tracts that were already outdated by the time I got
my hands on them in 1976 or so. Most lacked even the commitment to gayness I'd developed for myself. They just wanted
to be like everyone else, and unfortunately they were: normal
guys who happened to have sex with other normal guys. For
me, to be gay was an elective affinity, a chosen destiny. For
most of them, it was just something you did in the dark, in a
nightclub, or in a bedroom, and then you put on a suit and
went to the office, where you did important things.

I learned many useful things during my time in Boston, like
how to give attitude and how to read people cruelly but oh
so wittily, which make of Levi's showed off my ass to best
effect and which style of Doc Martens went with which belt:
knowledge that still stands me in good stead. But the main
thing I learned was that white gay men were a lot like other
white people, and as my mother told me some time ago, white
people stick together. In Boston, Chicago, and New York, when
you go out to gay clubs and gay youth groups and gay political
meetings and gay social groups, what you mainly meet are
white gay men, and what they're mainly looking to meet are
other white gay men, what queer theorist Richard Meyer (in
an utterly *other* context: Andy Warhol's, to be exact) calls the
desirable surface of sameness. Your average white gay man,

whatever his political identifications or inclinations, is white and a man long before he's gay, certainly when it comes to his allegiances to or disavowals of other gays who might not be sufficiently either.

Hub of educational activities that it is, Boston is also where I learned that I wasn't quite the transcendent individual I'd groomed myself to be. I was an individual to be sure (even when I didn't want to be), but I was a black individual, and that made a difference, both in the eyes of those around me and in my own eyes that had so long seen my face in the mirror as irremediably ugly. *But at least I was smart.* Which consolation didn't seem to be able to get me a job that paid more than one hundred and fifty dollars a week. As a friend once told me with the best of intentions, "You're always trying to make sure everybody knows you're smart, but nobody cares."

The revelation of my failed transcendence led me to ponder why it was that those two terms, individual and black, seemed so mutually exclusive. I can't count the number of "I don't think of you as black, I just think of you as a person" conversations I've had over the years: as if one couldn't possibly be both. Though *this* one obviously was and would continue to be. White people in general don't see black people as such (all black people, any black people) as people. Given that black people are also produced (literally) by this society, black people often don't see themselves and each other as people either. Despite my cherished monadic solipsism, I've hardly occupied some Archimedean point outside society. I have spent my whole life in pursuit of the chimera of personhood, individuality, *me:* free at last, black no more. Yet who I am, the *me* who so longed for an existence unfettered by labels, is exactly that black person who wants to stop being black, who developed such a "strong personality" in part to obscure his categorical blackness. A desire to escape one's social (and psychic) identity, one's *race,* after all rarely occurs to white people in this or any other country, wiggers and wannabes notwithstanding. For a white person to see me not as black, but as some race-lessly disembodied intelligence—an outcome that is the best one can hope for in a society so defined and deformed by race as this one, a consummation, indeed, most devoutly to be wished for—is for him not to see me at all, for the *self* I have so longed to be recognized to be erased. It is indeed a conundrum to both fervently wish to become and always already to be the invisible man, though the possibility of being no one at all has always appealed to me: except then I wouldn't get to be *me*.

In the so-called gay community, divided between white men who would never sleep with a black man and white men who slept only with black men (a *much* smaller group), I've experienced this same dissonance between who I thought I was and what I appeared to be (though obviously the two have been more intertwined in my own mind than I'd want to admit). There seems always to be a line, and I seem always to be on the wrong side of it, never sufficiently *us* to be one of the gang, never sufficiently *them* to be forbidden fruit. In both instances, my *self* keeps getting in the way. But which self? I've never been very good at being a sexual fetish, especially when I've tried, and being a snap queen isn't quite my forté either. Perhaps if I worked out more, and thought less . . .

The realization that one isn't exactly part of the gay community is even more problematic when one can hardly consider oneself part of a black community either, *any* black community. Given my social circumstances, I've simply never *known* many black people. And most of the black gay men in my immediate vicinity (not a large cohort) have been playing the same game I was, though most have seemed a bit more successful at it. *They* have seemed to experience no contradiction between their selves and their roles. Maybe they've played for lower stakes. (I've always gone for broke, selfhood or bust.) Maybe they've been better players. Maybe the grass is always greener.

I've also been afraid of "putting myself in touch" with the (imaginary) black community, because I've feared their disapproval and rejection, a rejection I've experienced all my life from those black communities with which I have had contact: Not so much because I was gay, but because I was, or was constantly told I was (by, for example, my mother's family), an oreo, without even the dignity of a capital O or registered trademark. Just walking past a group of (purportedly heterosexual) black men or boys on the street is an ordeal when one is marked by one's gait or one's clothes or one's speech as guilty of not being one of us, though one's skin color says one should be. Many black people seem all too eager to police one another's blackness, and certainly being gay (or rather, being openly and avowedly gay) can make one *entirely* not black enough. Homosexuality, at least the kind that dares to speak its name and introduce itself, is still in too many black people's eyes the white man's disease. Just ask Chuck D of the rap music group Public Enemy or Minister Louis Farrakhan. Better yet, don't.

Then there is the question of my bad object choice. Having experienced and come perhaps too much to expect a severe lack of welcome as an oreo, to what "home" could I expect to return (for the first time, no less) as a snow queen? There are certainly enough black gay people (or is it gay black people?) out there willing to inform me in no uncertain terms that *that* is the true white man's disease, and I've got a bad case. (There are, of course, also numerous white liberals who justify their distaste for black bodies by such alibis: It's a black thing, they wouldn't want to understand.) If I expect to come to that home, the House of Gay-Men-of-Suitably-Proud-African-Descent, it had better be with a suitably revolutionary black loved one in tow. Self-anointed Afrocentrism comes in several flavors, none of them to my taste.

Having spent my life as what journalist Hilton Als calls a Negro lost to other Negroes, and having had other Negroes participate eagerly in the process of my being lost to them, in the process of losing me as often and brutally as possible, I have developed a preemptive rage toward those other Negroes, who are all-too-tangible reminders of my own (by definition excessive) "blackness." It *is*, as they say, written all over my face, as on the faces of all the black people from whom I desperately try to distinguish myself: black boys who walk down the street with their mouths hanging open, wearing Raiders jackets, and black knit caps (mugger caps, we called them when I was young), who rap along with their headphones too loudly on the subway or sit there and nod like muppets to the beat. I am painfully and even obsessively alert to every way in which "those black people" (especially those black *men*) confirm stereotypes, for every "Yo blood, wussup!" reflects badly on *me*. I am not like them at all. I always carry a book on the train.

"Black" being is always being-for-other, never being-for-itself: And for blacks the "other" is black as well as white. ("Being-for-itself," in our society, is a mirage for *everyone*, but there are those allowed to believe they can reach that glittering oasis.) I measure constantly the distance I hope to achieve from other black people and the distance I can never bridge from other white people. Both blackness and whiteness are simulacra of what has never existed, but both for blacks and whites, to achieve the simulacrum of whiteness (a simulacrum of a simulacrum) is the mark of personhood, always erased before *I* get to make *my* mark. It is at least possible for "whites" to *believe* they have attained whiteness, while for "blacks" the impossibility of such an attainment gnaws at one night and day. Only black people have a race. The rest are just people.

I recall a conversation several years ago with a black university administrator (in charge of shepherding Negroes through the institution, as most are) in which she cut me off in the middle of some peroration about my hatred of white people to point out, "You don't hate them. You love them. We all do. We're just angry that they don't love us back." Indeed. I have all my life harbored an intense and unabated desire to *be* those privileged, pretty white boys I have always desired, those beautiful boys with whom I have enjoyed many an illusory intimacy (whiteness is no less abstract to me than blackness, though I do at least *know* white people). In the Latin poet Catullus's words, *Odi et amo*: I hate *and* love those boys, hate them precisely because they have never reciprocated my love, have perhaps never even recognized it as such; I've hidden it so well. I tell myself I hate them *because* of their whiteness (a mantle so unthinkingly assumed), their arbitrary power over my world. But even in my most solipsistic moments, I can't avoid wondering whether these things are actually the same, other than in my racialized imagination, my blocked identifications with an impossible (imaginary) object of desire. Is whiteness really beauty? Is beauty really power? Certainly all

white men, even all gay white men, are far from beautiful. But
then, no actual man could be as young and beautiful as my
imagoes. This power that Lucas and Jeremy, Jonathan and
Todd, and their lovely brothers have over me is a power of
which they remain largely unaware; they're only trying to get
laid, or just trying to cross the street. They are the *not-me* to
whom I have delegated the power to justify or negate me, a
power for which they never asked.

Those men and boys, however handsome or stylish, are
hardly representative, of whiteness, of maleness, or even (given
the outsized roles they play in the theatre of my psyche) of
their all-too-human selves. Yet still they represent so much for
me. The emotional power of which I spoke, as distinct from
whatever social privilege they may enjoy as Planter's Peanuts
heirs or investment brokers, is one that *I* bestow, and only on
the most beautiful. It's hardly fair to ask them to bear the
burden of my image-repertoire. I've known those men for
years, slept with many of them. (You didn't think I just sat at
home and counted my little fingers, did you, poor little boy
blue?) They're neither muses, myths, nor nightmares, just
young Caucasian males with good cheekbones and large clothing budgets. My projections are only ghost bodies (to adapt
the title of my ex-lover, the video artist Chris Cutrone's visual
meditation on the ambivalences of interracial desire), somewhat like mine, aftereffects of desire and deprivation.

The condition of being both too black and not black enough
is more or less the place, or lack of place (a nowhere, though
hardly a utopia), from which I write. The decentered self is a
notion deep in vogue among the intellectual circles in which I
move and hope to move, but the contradictions of being what
the postcolonial cultural theorist Homi Bhabha calls the other's
other (let alone the self's other) are far from theoretical.
Though I'm hardly interested in the one given identity on offer,
neither the same old white heterosexual male nor the same
new black heterosexual male, nor even the all new, improved
same black homosexual male (revolutionary desire included
for no extra charge), I keep hoping there'll be one better behind
door number four, five, or perhaps even six. . . . I'm still
counting.

The late videomaker Marlon Riggs spoke of the advantage that accrues from occupying no fixed social or cultural position: It keeps you from taking things for granted. But I feel mainly the lack of a place I can call my own, the absence of a space where I can take myself as a given. I'm constituted by that absence, it's made me what I am. But "Not this one. Nope, not that one either" has gotten tired and tiring, whether spoken in my voice or someone else's. While I can say along with Walt Whitman, "I am large, I contain multitudes," Mephistopheles's words in Christopher Marlowe's *Doctor Faustus* come just as immediately to mind. When asked just what he was doing out of hell (a question asked all to frequently, and with every possible inflection, of a black boy in the throes of what is jestingly called the higher education), he replied, "Why this is hell, nor am I out of it." Hell is other people. Hell is oneself. But the hell of knowing is infinitely preferable to the hell of not-knowing, or far worse the hell of pretending not to know, in which frozen inferno (Dante's, perhaps, or merely my own) I spent many a year with my head trapped under the ice, unable to breathe or to see. The question remains: Who's next?

THOUGHTS ON TRADE/ENDING AN OBSESSION

by Edwin L. Greene

The word "trade" is a slang term, origin unknown, used mostly by African-American gay men. It is used as a descriptive noun as in "That's a hot piece of trade" or "Is he trade?" or "Don't mess with my trade." In addition, it can be employed in either a singular or collective sense depending on context. I am familiar with the term "rough trade," but I don't think it applies here because the black gay men I've known don't pick up trade with the express desire to be brutally assaulted, although that and worse may happen during the course of the encounter. They are looking for hot sex (mostly oral and anal intercourse), and it goes without saying that trade can often turn out to be "rough." To be sure I clearly understood the term as it is used in black gay life, I asked several friends for their thoughts on the subject. I came up with this definition of trade: "straight" men who "mess around" (have sex) with gay men for some sort of compensation. Any trade worthy of the name has several girlfriends, some children, and maybe a wife in order to maintain his public heterosexuality. He takes the so-called male role in male-to-male sex, meaning he is the inserter in both oral and anal sexual activity. He feels he's doing the gay man a "favor" because in no sense does he consider himself gay or even bisexual.

Many African-American gay men of my generation (I am forty-one years old as this is written) and older have obsessively pursued sex and even "relationships" with trade. They have rejected less stridently masculine kinds of men. In most cities with significant black populations, there are clubs where trade and black gay men looking for each other mix. They are not necessarily identified as gay bars by their owners and patrons, but everyone knows what goes on. These clubs are often owned by straight whites even though the clientele is black (excluding those white gay men who frequent these bars because of their attraction to black men).

Trade usually won't live with a gay man because it's bad for that straight image. He comes around to have sex and leaves. He feels he should get paid for sex, if not in cash then maybe a meal will do. I have a friend, a university instructor, who used to live across the street from a shabby, mostly black, straight bar. He told me that over a period of years, he had sex with most of the men who frequented the club. He was an expert at "working" trade. He was also a great cook and when a man left his apartment, he was well fed.

Another way trade gets "paid" is when he's allowed to spend a night or two after being down on his luck or when he's having problems with his girlfriend (or wife). He'll stay only until the storm passes, which usually doesn't take long. One man said proudly that when he gets "cussed out" by one of his ladies, she calls within twenty-four hours to get him back. These men often think they are the ultimate ladies' man. They also tend to be very restless and don't believe in staying in one place too long.

In a moment of reflection, a middle-aged friend told me that most of his buddies (he was including himself, I believe) have never truly loved or been loved in their lives. All they've ever had in life is trade. It was an admission and a revelation. I have asked myself and others why so many black gay men spend years searching for that so-called straight man. I don't mean the occasional fantasy about hot sex with an attractive man who may or may not be straight. We've all done that. I'm referring to those black gay men who make an obsessive commitment to finding and "having" trade.

Years ago a straight woman friend took me to a party given by a gay friend of hers. She introduced us, thinking we might become an item. Later she told me (somewhat puzzled as well as amused) that he had confided to her that "Nothing was happening because two bitches can't do anything for each other." In other words, he was a "bitch" and so was I, as were all gay men.

To be gay then is to not be a man. Straight men or straight-acting men are the only men who count (this parallels the habit many gay men have of calling each other bitches, either in anger or in jest). Still, other black gay men have told me they could never relate to a gay friend as a lover. Why? "Because he's my sister." And sisterhood kills desire.

The trade mystique is fueled by several distortions. First, there is a misconception as to what a "real" man is. Many black gay men feel deeply that a man is someone unlike themselves. From this way of feeling comes the attempt by many gay men to re-create for themselves the traditional male (strong)/female (weak) relationship (many gay men speak urgently of wanting a "husband"), which doesn't work for straight couples, and so cannot possibly work for gays. Thirdly, there is a problem involving self-perception. Black gay men are extremely uncomfortable with their essential gayness. Most think being gay is wrong, sinful, and must never be revealed to any straight person, including family and friends. This is fertile ground for trade to exploit. It is within this context that many black gay men have pursued sexual and emotional fulfillment.

We are convinced from our social conditioning that we are wrong for being gay (weak, unnatural) so we, of course, think of our gay brothers the same way. Because of this way of thinking, most of us have extreme difficulty forming long-term stable relationships with each other. As my friend quoted above said, most of us never find lasting love because we don't want each other (we're not real men). We want so-called straight men (trade). A disastrous choice, as we shall see.

Let's say that a gay man finds the "real" man of his dreams. What does he do with his prize? Here is a likely scenario. If the trade eventually "gives up some good head" or "throws his legs up in the air" (which often happens), the gay man loses "respect" for his piece who has now "disgraced" his manhood and revealed himself to be just another sissy. At this point, the gay man will tell his friends, "I knew he was a woman." But why does it matter? Why not enjoy his sexual flexibility? If he lets his guard down and gives as well as receives, the gay man who is obsessed with the idea of trade will no longer see him as a real man. Interest suddenly vanishes, and the search begins anew for that perfect specimen of manhood. I have a sense that the word "straight," when applied to trade, really means straight-*acting*. A way of walking, talking, and just behaving that a certain kind of black man projects. Someone with little to offer except the appeal and excitement of his "street" masculinity. A poor black man's manhood.

Although I've never been attracted to trade in an obsessive way, I have an experience to share. Once back in the 1970s I picked up a guy one night and we drove to what he said was his residence. I parked, but before we could get out of the car, he pointed a gun in my face. He demanded all my money, which amounted to five dollars. This enraged him, and he said, "If this is all the money you got, I ought to blow your brains out." He ordered me out of my car and told me to lie on the ground while he searched my car for hidden valuables. When he found nothing, he said, "Where do we go to fuck?" I said, with the gun still pointed at me, "We're not going anywhere." He then wanted to know where I lived. At the time, I lived with my father. I told him I was not taking him to where I lived. For some reason, he then gave up and told me I could leave. Fortunately, I left the scene intact. Many have not been so lucky. I learned my lesson and never picked up a stranger again. I was not afraid during the ordeal, it was only afterward. While safe at home in my bed I began to imagine all the horrible possibilities of that encounter. It was then that I felt fear.

Remembering this experience brings to mind the many terrible stories I've heard involving gay men who were murdered by their trade during a "one-night-stand" or during the course of a "relationship." Gay men of my generation know well of what I speak. We have known many men who took the wrong one home or took him home one time too many. These murders have been particularly gruesome, involving multiple stabbings, shootings, and the severing of body parts, especially genitals. And we don't hear about the attacks that don't make the news because the victim wasn't killed. Actually, there are two problems here. The gay man's own self-hatred manifested as internalized homophobia and likewise the self-hatred and homophobia of the men we call trade. An often deadly combination. Trade is desperately determined to avoid the truth about themselves, which is they are either gay or bisexual. Knowledge they, along with gay collaborators, refuse to own. Black gay men have told me stories of trade they've had sex with who have either refused to acknowledge them or called them a faggot in public. These actions speak loudly of the deep contempt felt by trade toward gay men, especially ones they're having sex with. To make matters worse, the gay men so insulted most likely would have sex with the guy again at the next opportunity.

There are a number of ugly characteristics common to trade. They are irresponsible at best and dangerous at worst. They spend a lot of time plotting and engaging in criminal activity. They beat and rob gay men knowing their victims will probably not report them to the police for fear of being outed. Usually they don't hold jobs, or take care of their children or even themselves. Many can barely read and write. They are as likely to steal your VCR as have sex with you. I have seen professional gay men with seemingly a lot going for themselves end up destroyed by trade. I know a schoolteacher who became involved with crack during the course of his association with trade. He became a small-time seller and went to prison. Needless to say, he lost his job. While in prison, his crack "friends" cleaned out his apartment and his bank account. Now he exists on welfare and handouts, still addicted to trade and crack.

Many black gay men feud with one another over trade. I know a group of men, all over fifty, living in the same building, who are true believers in trade. These men are always in an uproar over who's having whose piece. Meanwhile, they're regularly being robbed of their possessions as well as played against each other. And they *still* keep these guys around.

Gay men who chase after trade are running after a discredited idea. Discredited because most gay men who have this obsession have suffered the physical, verbal, and emotional violence that comes with the territory. They're not even being sexually satisfied in the bargain. After all, trade will perform only the male (inserter) role in sex (if he wants to maintain the gay man's respect), so that leaves the gay man with a hard penis and no release.

In view of the perilous consequences of pursuing trade, what are some things African-American gay men should do? Hard as it may be, men, burn the "real" man ideal out of your mind. Define for yourself what a man is. Reject the prevailing homophobic stereotypes of manhood. No man is "more of a man" than any other man. Don't think some guy with a street manner or a certain physique is more man than you. Believe that someone like you is a man and is worth wanting. Also, we must not try to pattern our relationships after those of straight couples (as of this writing, 50 percent of heterosexual marriages end in divorce). Learn to love your gay self. Don't be ashamed of your sexual orientation. Homosexuality is not a choice or a lifestyle. It is a human condition fixed before one becomes sexually active. It cannot be changed by will. No one chooses to be gay any more than people choose to be heterosexual, brown-eyed, or African-American.

Fortunately, the idea of trade is beginning to die a natural death, particularly among younger black gay men, a victim, in part, of our rising self-esteem. Often as trade ages they gradually become more willing to experiment with sexual positions that they, in earlier years, would have rejected as "female" (gay). Also, because of the crack craze, trade will give head or give up the buns quicker than some gay man for five dollars or less. For most, this destroys the mystique that trade represents. And the AIDS epidemic, unfortunately, plays a part in the demise of trade, although I haven't yet figured it all out. I do know that black gay men with common sense are seriously re-evaluating their sexual priorities. Some still cling to the old ways. For so many middle-aged black gay men, trade is a bittersweet tradition.

Some readers may feel I've been too hard on trade and have portrayed gay men as innocent victims. The truth is, both groups have allowed a homophobic social order to dictate how they choose to fulfill their sexual natures. I realize that trade is sometimes victimized because of poverty and that they are usually younger than their gay male benefactors. However, gay men are the usual victims in the often violent power struggles between themselves and their trade. As a gay man myself, I'm sympathetic to my gay brothers.

As we explore our identities and *real* needs, we will begin to take better care of ourselves and one another. We must subject every aspect of our lives (both in and out of bed) to scrutiny and get rid of the bad, the ugly, the destructive, and the merely useless. And insist that our friends do the same. The obsessive pursuit of trade is intensely antigay as well as self-destructive. Is it asking my brothers too much to give up trade completely? For the true addict, easier said than done, I know. But consider the positive benefits. For starters, there is the freeing up of time needed to complete that advanced degree you never finished, or to help a friend living with HIV/AIDS.

Perhaps because of embarrassment, trade has been mostly ignored in the growing body of work by black gay male writers. There is no need for discomfort. Trade as a major driving force in black gay life deserves and demands serious study and comment.

Let's let the healing begin.

BROTHER TO BROTHER:
WORDS FROM THE HEART

by Joseph F. Beam

". . . what is most important to me must be spoken, made verbal and shared, even at the risk of having it bruised or misunderstood."

—AUDRE LORDE[1]

"I know the anger that lies inside me like I know the beat of my heart and the taste of my spit. It is easier to be angry than to hurt. Anger is what I do best. It is easier to be furious than to be yearning. Easier to crucify myself in you than to take on the threatening universe of whiteness by admitting that we are worth wanting each other."

—AUDRE LORDE[2]

I too know anger. My body contains as much anger as water. It is the material from which I have built my house: blood-red bricks that cry in the rain. It is what pulls my tie and gold chains taut around my neck, fills my penny loafers and my Nikes, molds my Calvins and gray flannels to my torso. It is the face and posture I show the world. It is the way, sometimes the only way, I am granted an audience. It is sometimes the way I show affection. I am angry because of the treatment I am afforded as a black man. That fiery anger is stoked additionally with the fuels of contempt and despisal shown me by my community because I am gay. *I cannot go home as who I am.*

When I speak of home, I mean not only the familial constellation from which I grew, but the entire black community: the black press, the black church, black academicians, and the black left. Where is my reflection? I am most often rendered invisible, perceived as a threat to the family, or I am tolerated if I am silent and inconspicuous. I cannot go home as who I am, and that hurts deeply.

Almost every morning I have coffee at the same donut shop. Almost every morning I encounter the same black man who used to acknowledge me from across the counter. I can only surmise that it is my earrings and earcuffs that have tipped him off that I am gay. He no longer speaks; instead he looks disdainfully through me, as if I were glass. But glass reflects, so I am not even that. He sees no part of himself in me— neither my blackness nor my maleness. Should our glances meet, he is quick to use his *Wall Street Journal* as a shield, while I wince and admire the brown of the coffee in my cup.

I do not expect his approval—only acknowledgment; the struggles of black people are too perilous and too pervasive for us to dismiss each other in such cursory fashion, because of perceived differences. Gil Scott-Heron called it "dealing in externals"; that is, giving importance to visual information and ignoring real aspects of commonality. Aren't all hearts and fists and minds needed in this struggle or will this faggot be tossed into the fire? In this very critical time everyone from the corner to the corporation is desperately needed.

> (Brother) the war goes on
> respecting no white flags
> taking no prisoners
> giving no time out for women and children
> to leave the area
> whether we return their fire
> or not
> whether we're busy attacking each other
> or not.
>
> —JULIE BLACKWOMON[3]

If you could put your newspaper aside for a moment, I think you too would remember that it has not always been this way between us. I remember. I remember the times before different

meant separate, before different meant outsider. I remember
Sunday school and backyard barbeques and picnics in the park
and the avenue and parties in dimly lit basements and skate-
boards fashioned from two-by-fours and B-ball and . . . I remember. I also recall secretly playing jacks and jumping rope
on the back porch, and the dreams I had when I spent the
night at your house.

But that was before different meant anything at all, certainly
anything substantial. That was prior to considerations such as
too light/too dark or good/bad hair, before college/army/jail,
before working/middle class, before gay/straight. But I am no
longer content on the back porch; I want to play with my jacks
on the front porch. There is no reason for me to hide. Our
differences should promote dialogue rather than erect new ob-
stacles in our paths.

> Dream 84: 15 February 1984
> We have all gathered in the largest classroom I have ever
> been in. Black men of all kinds and colors. We sit and talk
> and listen, telling the stories of our lives. All the things we
> have ever wanted to say to each other but did not. There is
> much laughter, but also many tears. Why has it taken us so
> long? Our silence has hurt so much.

On another day: I am walking down Spruce/Castro/Christo-
pher Street on my way to work. A half block away, walking
toward me, is another black gay man. We have seen each other
in the clubs. Side by side, at the precise moment our eyes
should meet, he studies the intricate detail of a building. I
check my white sneakers for scuff marks. What is it we see in
each other that makes us avert our eyes so quickly? Does he
see the same thing in me that the man in the donut shop sees?
Do we turn away from each other in order not to see our
collective anger and sadness?

The same angry face, donned for safety in the white world,
is the expression I bring to you. I am cool and unemotive,
distant from what I need most. "It is easier to be furious than
to be yearning. Easier to crucify myself in you." And perhaps

easiest to ingest that anger until it threatens to consume me, or apply a salve of substitutes to the wound.

But real anger accepts few substitutes and sneers at sublimation. The anger-hurt I feel cannot be washed down with a Pepsi or a Colt 45; cannot be danced away; cannot be mollified by a white lover, nor lost in the mirror reflections of a black lover; cannot evaporate like perspiration after a Nautilus workout, nor drift away in a cloud of reefer smoke. I cannot leave it in Atlantic City, or Rio, or even Berlin, when I vacation. I cannot hope it will be gobbled up by the alligators on my clothing, nor can I lose it in therapeutic catharsis. I cannot offer it to Jesus/Allah/Jah. So, I must mold and direct that fiery cool mass of angry energy—use it before it uses me!

Anger unvented becomes pain, pain unspoken becomes rage, rage released becomes violence.

Use it to create a black gay community in which I can build my home surrounded by institutions that reflect and sustain me. Concurrent with that vision is the necessity to repave the road home, widening it, so that I can return with all I have created to the home that is my birthright.

Note: This version of "Brother to Brother" was published in the *New York Native* (Issue 101), 22 October–4 November 1984.

NOTES

1. Audre Lorde, "The Transformation of Silence into Language and Action," *Cancer Journals* (Duluth, Minn.: Spinsters Ink, 1980).

2. Audre Lorde, "Eye to Eye: Black Women, Hatred, and Anger," *Sister Outsider* (Freedom, Calif.: Crossing Press, 1984).

3. Julie Blackwomon, "Love Poem for Sister Sonia," *Revolutionary Blues and Other Fevers* (self-published, 1984; distributed by Giovanni's Room, Philadelphia, Pa.).

· II ·
RELATIONSHIPS

Mentoring Gay Youth

by *Thom Bean*

When I came out in Chicago, I was the Eve Harrington or "poor relation" to a circle of gay decorators, designers, and otherwise prominent men. I was plain in accomplishment. But youth has its physical promise. Like many social circles, a little bait on the hook makes parties more interesting. Also, well-spoken blacks were fashionable then. I was young enough to be impressed by names, addresses, and titles. I liked being taken, as long as it wasn't too lightly. I didn't use drugs, was never drunk, and didn't sleep at the opera. I just needed guidance, direction, hope.

W. H. Auden at thirty-two had a relationship with eighteen-year-old Chester Kallman, which lasted thirty-four years.

At eighteen, I would sneak into gay bars. An older man would send me drinks and dance around while holding a drink over my head. This older man, as it turned out, was from a prominent family, was a diva in the pre-Stonewall gay social circuit, a successful businessman, and a wonderful, gracious person. We'll call him Jaguar Bob. Jaguar Bob had two things I still don't have: wealth and power.

He gave me advice, support, and direction as well as lent me office space, a phone to use, and support when I was unemployed. He took me to dinner, listened to my problems, took me under his wing in his social circle, and provided space for me to grow as a gay man. Jaguar Bob's only wish was that I pass on the favor to others "When the time is right." But the gay political and social climate has changed. Jaguar Bob is a dinosaur, and mentoring is on its last gasp. Mentoring can be a two-edged sword. If the mentor or the protégé is not careful, mentoring can turn into a hustle, danger, or even death. Neither the hunter nor the hunted is always what he seems. Remember the serial killer Jeffrey Dahmer?

This thought occurred to me as I was watching *Six Degrees of Separation*, a must-see movie. The movie's central character is a bright BGM desperately in search of mentoring. Being poor, black, and gay excludes him from his vision of success. His options are limited. The rules are meant to exclude those not empowered to change the rules. The white New York City bluebloods found him to be an anomaly, an amusing anecdote for dinner parties and theatre intermissions. The difference between the haves and the have-nots was shown as a two-sided Russian Modern painting by Kandinsky. One side was entitled *Control*, the other side, *Chaos*. The Ruling Class has control. The Ruled are condemned to chaos.

Oscar Wilde's undoing was at the age of thirty-seven when he began his nine-year relationship with Lord Alfred Douglas, who at the time was twenty-one.

These are hard times to find a clean-cut protégé as Jaguar Bob found in me thirty years ago. We were both lucky. Nowadays, gay youth gravitate toward the fast lane. Many are consumed by drugs, sex, and self-importance before learning anything about all they can be. Many are not interested in anything beyond the moment. They can't remember and don't care about anything complicated. They wish only to escape from problems not easily resolved, risks not easily taken. Many don't trust anyone outside their social circle or age group. Mentoring is a two-way commitment.

Leonardo da Vinci at thirty-eight mentored a ten-year-old street urchin nicknamed Salai. Despite the fact that Salai was a thief and a scoundrel, they remained together almost twenty-six years.

In the 1960s, there were quaaludes instead of AZT. There was no AIDS. Relatively carefree sex existed—with an occasional case of the drip (gonorrhea). There were no guns in school. Youth were not sick and dying at alarming rates. Graffiti and gangs did not prevail. Homelessness was an occasional "bum," not the legions of people we see today. Where are the mentors for people who fall through the cracks? Is criminalizing not being a white employed heterosexual a better investment than providing equal opportunity? How many have-nots can this society afford to shut out, put on entitlement, or incarcerate? Is it better to warehouse those for whom there are no viable choices? Society is scared of choices between consenting adults, classes, races, sizes, sexes, and age groups. Mentoring could help where law enforcement cannot.

Walt Whitman at forty-six began his eight-year relationship with Peter Doyle, who was eighteen.

Some mentoring is platonic, some romantic. Some mentoring occurs because of physical attraction. So what? Isn't caring with sex better than sex without caring? Some of us end up with neither. The oldest profession occasionally produces mentor/protégé relationships. Three Roman emperors (Domitian, Octavius, and Elagabalus) did it for money while youths. I know a prominent man who was once a call boy and whose lover was married. The chemistry was right. There was a divorce. The wife struck out. Now the two men are both rich and happy! Do miracles come true? In their case, yes. The nurturing from mentors who understand what the protégé is going through seems to help. Sex was better when it was not as commercial as it is today. Nowadays, gays identify sexually more so than they do spiritually. Gays tend to think of each other in terms of sexual value.

André Gide at forty-seven mentored sixteen-year-old Marc
Allégret. They enjoyed a long relationship. Allégret became
an important film director.

A homo punk observed: "Young homo punks I know move
to London, New York City, or San Francisco to find audience
and support for being outrageous. These are cities where we
know we can find others who are going through the same
process." This homo punk noted his social circle is all young,
white, working class or middle class, and from a similar suburban background as his own. "They may look punked out, but
they are still white suburban Wonder Bread inside. We don't
interact with different ethnic groups or cultures so much. We
listen to our own music (white) and do our own thing."

Hadrian, a bearded Roman emperor, at forty-eight began a
six-year love affair with Antinous, who was only fifteen.

Curiosity about difference has changed. If I had only sought
out men who looked like me, if I had been too scared to expand my prospects, I would have missed some of the most
significant parts of my life. It is one thing to adopt affectations
and quite another to explore new and diverse possibilities.
That is how we grow. Not by sticking to the safe, predictable
route approved by people who are just as afraid of differences
as we are. Through mentoring and exploring differences, we
define who we are; we learn to interact in a pluralistic society.
By being monocultural, Americans are less prepared to interact
within the larger global community. We must make monocul-
turalism an embarrassment, if not a sin. The mentoring process
helps us explore and transcend boundaries. The Racialists and
Religious Right are mentoring their young. They are passing
on the seeds of oppression by training their children to hate.
They are becoming more restrictive and better organized while
gays are weakening from less interaction and mentoring.

At forty-eight Christopher Isherwood began a relationship
with eighteen-year-old Don Bachardy, which lasted thirty-
two years.

Without mentoring, gays are not prepared to make life choices enjoyed by heterosexuals. Many gays emulate heterosexual patterns and aren't prepared to accept new definitions. Mentoring is like adopting with an option on long-term responsibility. Often, the most privileged children rebel against the efforts made by parents. With mentoring, those who choose to participate in a relationship have already chosen their roles. We cannot choose parents; however, we can choose our mentors.

At fifty-seven Rock Hudson began his four-year relationship with twenty-nine-year-old Marc Christian.

For whom does mentoring apply? Which of us needs no one to turn to? I get the impression that both gays and nongays think gay relationships are frivolous and not as important as their heterosexual counterparts. For some gay men, marriage to a woman is what they feel obliged to do to make themselves acceptable to their families, coworkers, and friends. Everyone must find out where they belong and what they have to do to get there for themselves. I learned people do not have value not because of who they are, but because of what they stand for. A lot of the people I thought were so important mean less now. We all learn early in life who we are supposed to be less than. We each must decide to what extent it is true; to what extent we will sacrifice our dreams and assume the assigned position. I'm glad I had a mentor like Jaguar Bob to tell me: "Fuck that shit!"

At thirty-nine Beauford Delaney, a portrait painter, began a thirty-nine-year relationship with James Baldwin, who was sixteen.

Without getting cosmic, I believe each of us has a responsibility to teach, to guide, to support, to learn as best we can. Through mentoring, the young benefit from the experience and guidance of the old, and the old benefit from the energy and the new perspectives of the young.

My loan from Jaguar Bob is due. Applications are now being considered.

I HATE BASKETBALL

by Kevin McGruder

It was an endurance test. Both physical and mental. I was playing basketball. I hate playing basketball. I was playing this game under duress as part of a Big Brothers program. My Little Brother and I were teamed against another Big and Little for a game of street ball. To make matters worse, I felt like I was coming down with something, but I didn't want to back out of the game, which had been planned for over a week, for fear of disappointing my Little Brother (or looking weak). As I huffed and puffed around the court missing shots and failing to snag rebounds, I knew that one of the reasons I hate to play basketball is because I play so poorly. As an African-American male, I admit this with a certain hesitancy, a slight feeling that I have let down the race; and as a gay man, I admit this with the feeling that I'm confirming a stereotype of nonathletic "sissies." But I love to play most sports. I just don't like playing basketball.

Now my dislike for playing basketball is not an irrational hatred, and it goes beyond my fear of having my ineptitude exposed. My dislike can be traced to a collision of the "honeyed lies of youth" with the bitter experiences of childhood. When I was in fifth grade, I was on a basketball team at my school. One evening I arrived at practice to discover something called "second cuts." I don't remember how the coach explained this novel concept to us, but I do remember that this was the first time he had mentioned it. A few minutes later I was gathering my things for the trip home, along with a few other unfortunates. The agony of defeat. And so began my ambivalence with organized sports. But I didn't give up on the basketball team right away. I asked my father to take me to all their games (which he did), where I would sit and watch, harboring the fantasy that somehow the team would run through all their reserves and need someone to fill in, and I would come down from the stands to save the game. Of course, this never happened, and if it had I wouldn't have been prepared (no uniform, no sneakers), but that's the joy of the fantasies of a ten-year-old boy.

Most of the heart-to-heart talks that I had with my father when I was growing up were centered around sports, and I remember him telling me that if I really wanted to play basketball, I would have to practice more. Soon I joined a team at church. I went through the season with them, but I just never got interested again.

Some of these thoughts went through my head while I was playing with Big Brother/Little Brother two-on-two game. No wonder I was missing shots and rebounds. Early in the game I had pretty much conceded to a switch in the student-teacher relationship between my Little Brother and me. Since he's a much better player than I ever was or will be, I gave him a chance to play the role of his hero, Michael Jordan. I fed him the ball and he made the shots. The Little against whom he was teamed was not as skilled. And I felt pangs of recognition as I heard his Big Brother criticize the weakness of his game. The Big Brother didn't say anything about my game or lack thereof. But every time he missed a shot while I was guarding him, his expression said, How could I miss a shot with this chump guarding me? Ah, the joys of street ball.

Sometimes I do wonder how different my life would have been if I had been proficient in the rough and tumble of street ball. I certainly would have developed some different personality traits. I'm too shy and thin-skinned for the street game, which is filled with banter and insults usually countered with displays of skill that silence the offender. But when your skills are minimal, what do you do? Respond with repartee? "Too bad you don't spend as much time learning your times tables as you do playin' ball" does not go over well on the court, although in my day I did use variations on this theme. I felt like reviving some of these old retorts as I listened to my Little Brother, obsessed with basketball, ask me why I missed a shot, and I wished that he could transfer a portion of that enthusiasm to schoolwork.

Arthur Ashe said that African-American youth spend too much time on the playing fields and not enough time in the classroom. I agree, but I do understand my Little Brother's enthusiasm for basketball. Even more than during my "wonder years" (the 1960s), proficiency at basketball these days is a primary barometer of manhood for many urban African-American youth. In many communities it is about the only "legit" barometer, a welcome alternative to fighting, drug dealing, and using guns. The respect earned by a good ballplayer is automatic. It's hard to knock something that has the power to give young boys confidence in themselves. And so I don't, but I do try to encourage my Little Brother to develop some of the other talents he has. While basketball may be the weapon of choice in making his way through the 'hood, I know he'll have to develop some other skills/weapons to make it in the outside world.

After my own ill-fated childhood experiences with basketball, I focused on school and music (I played the trombone). But I didn't give up on sports. It was the track team in junior and senior high school that made me feel like I was one of the guys. And I know playing basketball well gives my Little Brother the same feeling.

A lot of these thoughts swirled through my head as I sat resting after two games of ball. The other Big Brother had by this time gotten into a pickup game with the big boys on the other court. I was just glad that the games were over and that I hadn't died of a heart attack playing something that I don't like. After I had caught my breath, the two Little Brothers coaxed me into a less-competitive sport that is one of my favorites—we got on the swings.

GIL'S STORY

by Sur Rodney (Sur)

Tall, black, and handsome, Gil Rankin, a native of White Plains, New York, had lived in Paris for the last sixteen years. He was the first black figure skater to perform with Holiday on Ice and the Ice Capades.

Handling the crazy Frenchmen in his love life and trying to make a living in Paris were not easy tasks. Those Frenchmen couldn't keep their hands off him. His striking good looks, shaved head, goatee, tall and athletically muscular body, and café au lait complexion with dark piercing eyes turned many heads. Gil's *savoir faire* added to the appeal, especially with that gorgeous body. His performance years numbered, he began teaching privately with the hope of eventually starting his own production company. Despite his difficult life, and tumultuous love affairs, Gil was persistent. And working for his higher self, he knew that somewhere in the struggle he would accomplish his goals. It was only a matter of time.

Gil and I were birds of a feather. We came from a dance background, traveled extensively in Europe, and shared many similar experiences with life and love as gay black brothers. We began to form a bond through our regular correspondence with each other over the next year. We preferred and enjoyed writing letters. Although Gil was in no rush to visit New York often, if ever again, during the summer of 1990 the death of his father brought him back to the city.

There was no real love lost between Gil and his father. Returning to New York was something he would have preferred to avoid, especially when he was to experience difficulties with a problem cousin who had been appointed executor of his father's estate. "My father never thought my sister or I could handle financial responsibility as well as my seemingly professional and brilliantly educated cousin," I remember him telling me. "I don't know what my father was worried about, he never really had any money. A small ordinary house, an old run-down seventies Buick, and a bank account that would barely cover his taxes, burial, and legal fees." The problem cousin was eventually found out—he had a crack cocaine addiction. The situations that ensued throughout turned into a circus, something else that caused Gil to express a great deal of anger and frustration, while still holding on. "Would he have been able to deal with this without so many, many years of living in Paris?" I wondered. "Was this what he had been preparing for all these years?" His proceeds from the sale of the house and car were to be split with his sister. He had hoped this small sum of money would afford him an opportunity to rent his own apartment and begin to realize his longtime dream of starting his own production company. As could be expected, Gil had to return to Paris to settle his differences with an old boyfriend, who was becoming a bit too obsessed. Or was it an ex-lover of an ex? The story was a wild one, but the details of it fail me at the moment.

Soon after his return to Paris, Gil once again fell in love. This one, unlike the others, was special. He knew it with all his heart. Their lovemaking was different and so was his special talent. Jean-Marc was a skater, one of the rare special dancers on ice whose talents he believed could be trained to perfection. Jean-Marc was a natural—but still young, maybe a bit too young for the forever commitment of love. "I know he wants it, but is he ready to handle it?" Gil would ask. "He's too spoiled, and he demands constant attention. He was an only child. We're linked psychically. We have the same dreams at exactly the same times."

Somewhere in the midst of this love affair and transatlantic calls to lawyers mishandling his cousin's executor responsibilities, Gil decided to return to New York. "I've been having trouble with my balance, and a numbness in my left leg. I've been given some medication for it in Paris, but it still seems to be a problem. I will have to talk to my doctor in Paris to see what I can have done while I'm here. They have different names for diagnosis in French. Jean-Marc is worried and thinking I'm holding something back. When his mother died, he never quite got over it. I think he has great fears of losing me. By avoiding me, he does not have to deal with it." "Have you been tested?" I inquired. His condition sounded "toxo" symptomatic to me. I didn't want to diagnose his condition and strongly advised him to get tested, explaining that it might have an effect on his treatment and prescribed medications should he need any additional ones. Fortunately for him a family friend and nurse was able to guide him through the necessary channels and avoid unnecessary delays. This served as somewhat of a relief, but it did not stop my concern.

The next phase was a blur: doctors, clinic appointments, and his eventual admittance to the hospital. "Yes, I tested positive for HIV. What does that mean? How will Jean-Marc deal with it? What about Jean-Marc? Why won't he return my calls?" Gil was becoming obsessed with speculation about how this nonresponse by Jean-Marc could be interpreted. His worries were temporarily put on hold when he was admitted to the hospital to have lesions on his brain drained. Somehow I expected he was busy settling business in White Plains when really he was recovering in the hospital. The stories that ensued were a testament to a miraculous recovery. "I think they may have been wrong with their diagnosis." Denial sets in. "I was fine and started to get worse being in the hospital. I surprised them by recovering more quickly than they'd expected. Bringing in teams of interns and holding seminars by my bedside and every other day wanting to do more unnecessary tests. They were keeping me there as a guinea pig. They had a healthy body to experiment on! When the fevers started for no reason, I decided to get out of there. Enough is enough. I was exposing myself to something in there. And do you know as soon as I got away from there, the fevers stopped."

Gil sounded great. I wanted to see him. He complained of weakness and weight loss from spending so much time in the hospital. He needed to gain his weight back so he was eating six meals a day and slowly beginning to exercise. Anxious to see him, I set up a lunch date. It took a while for him to accept. His vanity was behind this, as I was to find out. He was bothered by his body and the slight scar on his head as a result of the draining. Although the doctors had done a remarkable job stitching up the opening and leaving, once healed, a minor scar and a slight indentation. Hardly enough to ruin his continued preference for shaving his head (his trademark). Worse yet, he had arrived in summer and was admitted in the fall. It was now winter, and he had no winter clothing. There was shopping to do. His packed closets were still in Paris. However, he needed only essentials.

On the day he arrived for lunch, he was hatless. I was shocked. It was cold. The vanity again. He said he didn't like the way he looked in a hat. We'd go to movies, have dinner occasionally, and talk about Jean-Marc. "Why hasn't he called? What does this mean? He wouldn't totally abandon me because he still has my skates!" The estate settlement was tied up in court, so his time was preoccupied with getting healthy again. And trying to make sense of Jean-Marc's behavior. Within months he was again looking terrific. Something that gave him great confidence and interest in pursuing two very important tasks at the moment. First, getting back to Paris and finding Jean-Marc. "I'm convinced that once he sees me or hears that I am back in Paris and looking great, he'll get over whatever he's going through and communicate." The second thing was taking note of the men on the street who seemed to do double takes on street corners or while stepping on or off subway cars. This obvious desire for him affirmed his full recovery and, to his detriment, strengthened the denial. He didn't keep his clinic appointments and rejected his medications. "The medications throw my equilibrium off. I'm an athlete. I know my body. I can't deal with feeling off balance. I function better without it. When I get back to Paris, I'll get my doctor to give me something. I trust the French doctors. Their approach to medication is much more balanced. They are not so quick to jump in on this AIDS treatment. Most American doctors are fools."

Gil started visiting bars and drinking alcohol. I called it reckless endangerment; he called it testing his limits. During one of his daytime strolls on the avenue, he'd met someone who'd become infatuated with him and coincidentally happened to be French. He was a chef in some Midtown hotel. Gil's involvement with him came to a halt when one day this guy just disappeared. He never returned Gil's calls. Gil couldn't understand why or what had happened to cause such an unexpected reaction. I could only guess.

Again, the issue with Jean-Marc would come to the surface. "I won't be able to rest until I know and understand for real what is in this crazy Frenchman's head. It has been more than a year. I've even sent him money I owed and never so much as received a confirmation. Now that's entirely out of character." Gil was beginning to worry more than ever. Something was wrong. A piece of the puzzle was missing. The disappearance of his new friend, his confusion about Jean-Marc, and the delays in settling his father's estate became too much. The stress was making him sick. He had come down with a cold that he couldn't get rid of. He was becoming such a wreck, he wasn't able to hold down any food. What an awful stomach flu, he thought. He refused to go back to the hospital. He wanted only to go back to Paris as soon as he felt better.

He never got back to Paris. He was rushed to the hospital at the insistence of his host, his old friend Bill with whom he'd been staying. Originally it was to be three weeks. It was now three months past a year. Bill was not one to baby-sit. He'd suspected Gil wasn't taking his medication. I knew he wasn't, too. What I didn't know was how much weight he had lost and how immobile he'd become before entering the hospital dehydrated. He was also beginning to have difficulty with his speech. I recall his difficulty having a conversation with me during this time. He would make it seem as though he was just too tired to talk at the moment, or he'd not answer the phone at all. Within minutes of his arrival at the hospital, they had him hooked up to everything. Within days his speech had deteriorated rapidly, and eventually he slipped into a coma. I was shocked when I visited him that Fourth of July weekend in 1992. His eyes were distant, his body fragile, his breathing labored. Trained athletes have an amazing capacity for the

body to take over and fight longer than what one might nor-
mally expect under such circumstances. I placed my hands on
his forehead to give him my blessings. "You can go now. It is
okay to let go. You are too brave and much loved. It's okay
to let go. You haven't failed us. We won't forget you. Go peacefully toward the light." Gil died the following morning.

The day his family gathered was a day I had planned to be
out of the city. I didn't change my plans. They never saw him
in the hospital before he died. The family was never really
ready to deal with Gil. How would they even begin to deal
with me. Would I only be another one to add to their confused
understanding and become the brunt of their disgust? I didn't
really want to take that chance. I didn't think it was my place.
Today I regret it.

Who in Paris or anywhere else for that matter will ever
know what happened to Gil Rankin? He never told any one
of his friends in Paris of his diagnosis or hospitalization for
fear that they would imagine only the worst. No one had any
contact with his Parisian friends or life. I think they preferred
not knowing. His address book is kept by some family member
who has yet to contact me or anyone else as far as I know.
His obituary has yet to be written.

A friend of the family had at one time expressed interest in
writing a biography of Gil's professional skating career. The
project was delayed. According to Gil, this friend, when finally
questioned about the delay, was forced to confess to having
problems with his homosexuality and his AIDS diagnosis. She
had recently found religion. I know nothing of his career. I
hope one day the full story of Gil Rankin, the first black figure
skater to dance and tour professionally with a major company,
will be told.

BEHIND THESE PRISON WALLS

by Eugene Harris

Within the steel walls of prison, a man must be strong mentally and physically or he will perish. It is a daily chore to get up and not know if it will be your last day because you may be in the wrong place at the wrong time. Plus, one must use extreme caution when dealing with the guards. Their mentality can make life a living hell if they want to. First, to be deprived of your freedom, loved ones, etc., has a psychological effect that can be compared to living in a vacuum. Then you must deal with the cold realization that this prison environment fills up the vacuum completely. To survive, one must be witty and use finesse.

As I do my time, I have had to earn respect here, both verbally and physically. In the joint, those who stand up as a man will either attain that respect, regardless of his sexual preference, or die. That is the cold fact of prison life.

Being behind bars one gets used to the screams of different inmates either getting raped or having a head-shattering orgasm by his own hand. If a gay person is "married," it usually grants him more respect and less headaches because he will rely on his "husband" for protection from adversaries. The "husband" will have some pull within the system, if he is lucky. Most guards still look upon the obviously feminine gay man as a joke, one to be low-rated and disrespected. In the hierarchy of prison life, gays are truly at the bottom. Now and then I can use eye-to-eye contact to find a closeted gay officer who may try to make life a little more comfortable for me and those other gays within his reach.

But then again, a cop might come into your room and tell you to let him suck your big dick. If you refuse, they will make your stay in prison rougher than it already is. So you have no choice but to let them have their way. You just lay back and feed them the thang and later enjoy the privileges of having extra cigarettes or extra food. Then, too, the cop will look the other way when you are in the wrong.

Everybody in the joint knows what's going on, but everybody denies it. In the end, the extra favors let me accept the reality that I have to give up the dick. It's especially hard for the new guys during their first week. It's really hard on them to have to do this and do that with cops they can't stand. You never know when sexual favors will be demanded of you. They may come back to their cell and find some commissary items on the bed, unaware that if they eat the items or use them in any way, they have just accepted part payment for a sexual encounter of any variety that the gift giver desires!

Being confined tends to build one's nature up constantly as a result of the lack of sex and the consumption of so much starchy food. I know my dick gets hard if the wind blows. Many lonely nights, when there is nothing to do, you hold your manhood in your hand and play with it, all the while fantasizing and knowing that you got the stamina and the endurance to shoot two or three times, releasing the sweet juices that are boiling within. Prison life and the sexual game is a twenty-four-hour reality.

During my many incarcerations, I have had associations with a lot of different gay males. I have rarely met one who has done a violent crime. Usually they are locked up on theft, drug sales, or burglary charges. The few violent ones usually had some type of domestic violence conviction. Overall, I find that the typical gay male inmate to be nonviolent. The gay men, for the most part, have a circle of friends in here, both for moral support and for the security of not being the only one. While here in prison, I witnessed the murder of two gays. One was killed by his jealous lover; the other was killed by a gangster who just couldn't stand faggots.

Despite the stigma of homosexuality, the s
try to buy sex from a gay male inconspicuou
friends, he will at all costs maintain his mucho
For example, he might get his homies on the s
him copies of *Playboy, Hustler, Velvet,* or some othe   .1es
with naked women. He might also protect his m. .v image
by saying, "Oh, I just did it (have a blowjob) a couple times.
I had to get my dick sucked, but I don't really fuck with
punks!" What a contradiction of action and words! In order to
understand the gay male, you can always go to the prison
library where books are available that help you to understand
their lives.

The few officers who are gay give a bad impression of gays
to the majority of inmates. They are reckless at times. When a
straight inmate doesn't want to submit to his advances, the
guard makes it hard on the inmate. In turn, the inmate will
take it out on any femme gay male inmate who shows any
kind of weakness.

Due to the outbreak of AIDS in the prison system, a scourge
that has risen to a staggering proportion, the obvious femme
gay male is looked upon as its cause. And that's one of the
main reasons for their stigmatization now. The medical administration doesn't even inform anyone if it is found out that he
is infected with the virus. They let the infected person circulate
within the general prison population until he gets sick and has
to stay at the infirmary. Since the state doesn't pass out condoms, they are allowing a lot of people to be infected with
HIV unnecessarily. Prison officials are aware that anal sex is a
common thing behind bars. I am aware, of course, that condoms don't give you 100 percent security, but it would lessen
the threat of catching AIDS, since approximately 85 percent of
the sex in prison is anal. For straight guys, especially to guys
who have thirty years or more to go before they become eligi-
ble for parole, a shot of ass can be addicting. And since 30
percent of the time the anal sex is not voluntary, the nondistri-
bution of condoms expresses the prison administration's total
disregard for the safety and well-being of the inmates in
their care.

As a black man confined to the crude world of incarceration, has inspired me to take advantage of the opportunity to earn my GED and to read voraciously. Only recently have I acknowledged myself, the real me as well as my potential and versatility. So for those of you who are out there in the free world, I leave you with this thought: Prison life, especially for the black gay man, is truly cruel and unusual punishment. And the criminal justice system is heartless and uncaring, with no rights for the incarcerated. Prison life is a living hell. Stay out!!!

Closets

by G. Winston James

Not since C. S. Lewis's *The Lion, the Witch, and the Wardrobe* has there been a wardrobe with so many exciting and dangerous adventures as the common closet of gay black life—our dark world of secret sharers. Many of us awakened to this closeted life in a small way as children—masturbating in secret with our little boy friends, or simply counting the number of pubic hairs that had grown since the last time we had compared the sizes of our penises. Children's closets, though, are so safe. Safe because they are so often not just clandestine meeting places, but also shared spaces of naïveté and discovery. Active denial comes later in life. It is only when we find ourselves curious about our fathers' penises and our brothers' penises that we begin to realize that it was not only friendship and budding boyhood that drove us into the intimate spaces in which we found ourselves with Tommy or John, but that there was also desire evolving in those tight little corners. "Perversion."

By the time we had pressed our eyes against a keyhole for the fifth time or hidden under our third bed waiting to catch sight of an adult phallus, we had almost certainly begun to consider our unspeakable curiosity alone. We had begun to isolate ourselves within our own personal closets from which several possibilities emerged: (1) our curiosity would subside naturally, (2) we would accept the views of society and actually suppress our desires (potentially to the detriment of our mental and emotional health), (3) we would come to understand our desires as needs and natural drives, and we would emerge from hiding, or (4) we would expand our closets as we matured, creating a somewhat socially acceptable hybrid of the second and third choices above; that is, we would choose to remain emotionally, socially, and politically immature and underexpressed so that we could live out our lives in a false security closely akin to that of our boyhoods. It is by electing choice number four that we have succeeded in creating our own communal closet, complete with all of the trees, tearooms, cheesy clubs, anonymous sex, and secrecy that make a clandestine life interesting and unfulfilling.

I think back to my earliest years of homosexual activity: I was four years old and already aware of the possibilities of the penis. I had had erections but thought that I was the only person on Earth who was able to produce them. I used to tell everyone I was magic; that is, until I played show-and-tell with my best friend from next door. He was also able to become erect and gave me my first chance to explore sex. Little did he know that I was already adept at manipulation. I utilized a series of "I dare you to dare me to" to get him to let me touch his penis, then put it in my mouth, then to touch his behind, and finally to kiss it. All this in a pantry surrounded by flour, canned goods, cereal, and darkness. When we emerged from that "closet," we left our secret inside. We never discussed that experience between us.

Nowadays, I frequent peep shows and have been to "safer-sex clubs," which are not unlike the pantry in my parents' first home. Little worlds that straight (and sometimes gay) men create to allow gay men to pretend to be free. Halls lined with books, booths, benches, and sex paraphernalia to absorb the sounds of our whispered conversations of sex. These are expensive games of hide-and-seek, show-and-tell, and truth-or-dare. See a man, cruise a man, touch a man, and dare yourself to fuck a man, but do not ask his name because he may lie to you, or worse, ignore you. Worse yet, he may tell you the truth and introduce responsibility into this bleak picture. He may actually like you and want to walk outside with you. But do you dare, since you probably didn't want to know his name in the first place? It is one thing to relish a man's penis—

sex is easy—and totally another to look into his mind and be concerned for anything beyond that sex.

When I was seven and living at a different address, a fifteen-year-old white boy on the block asked my sister and me if we would like to see his "cock." I don't recall what we responded at the time, but later, when he and I were alone, I said, "Yes." John and I then walked into a wooded lot behind one of the factories down the hill, pushing the branches out of our way and being careful not to rub our clothes on the drums of purple dye that had been discarded there. Then he showed me his penis. It was big and I thought "Nice," but then he was fifteen, and I was so small and curious.

"Touch it," he said. I reached out and touched it, and he showed me how to stroke it. I was enthralled. "Why don't you put it in your mouth? Go ahead. Just suck on it a little bit." I did. This was the first day that I'd performed fellatio on a "man" and the first time I'd seen a penis ejaculate. I felt as if I'd won a prize.

Understandably then, after I had come to New York years later, from ages seventeen through nineteen, I looked for John in every white boy bar I could find. I had been imprinted. His was the standard of beauty I pursued for the first years of my newly closeted life. Unlike most snow queens, however, since I was very black culturally-identified, I had to actively cultivate an attraction to their ways of socializing. Dressed in my preppy best, I met no white men, though, who did not soon find their way to their knees in front of me. The dynamic had changed. That made it easier for me to realize that these men were not John, that their world was foreign to me, and that I was a black man who had still not dealt with his own attraction for other black men.

During those years, I consciously attempted to hide myself in the closet of the white gay world, but found that my baggage did not allow me to fit in. Today I realize that I was not only beguiled by white men, but I was frightened of my own. Black men were too close to what I am. They were too close to the truth when what I was looking for was a new reality— one that did not overly remind me of the times when a relative and I played barber and I relished the feel of his hands.

Or of the time when he allowed me to fondle his erect penis and to rub it against my face under the sheets. Just as I had worked up the courage to suck it, he asked, "Are you a fag?" Instantly, I said "No," and let his penis rest where it lay— never to touch it again.

I cannot help but wonder whether, had my encounter with my relative been a more positive one, it would have taken me less time to become comfortable with other black men, as opposed to deluding myself that only the openness and liberality of white men could enable me to be free. I regret that my relative did not ask me if I wanted to eat his dick, because I am sure that I would have slept midway down the bed under the sheet for years. That way, perhaps, I could be looking back now and pretending that we shared trust and closeness, even though such times would have been only his private getting-off and my undercover submission.

That is how many of us are most comfortable anyway: when we are hidden, sexual, and allowing someone else in one way or another to direct our lives. We question, but our queries are cut short by humping, or the necessity to drop yet another quarter, or the nearby snap of a twig. We have stretched the fantasy of our surreal worlds, our closet lives, and have forced ourselves to believe that this is living. What is it that I should want from this "life?" If the moonlit handsome man who approaches one of us through the trees in Brooklyn's Prospect Park says, "You are beautiful. Why don't you let me fuck you?" some of us may think he cares. Maybe if we hear it enough times, and listen to the stories from our ki-ki's,[1] we will become convinced that there is no difference between intimacy and anonymous sex, and who needs relationships when you can be loved all of the time. Who needs quality time when you can be pressed up against 120 black men in an eighty-occupancy bar, with music so loud you can hardly hear yourself speak, let alone be expressive? Do we really need to delve into who we are?

I escaped my parents' pantry, the bushes behind factories, and the catacombs of Uncle Charlie's Bar, only to find that I and the other members of the gay black life are continually imposing boundaries on our world, building so many closets.

You may be gay in Keller's Bar, but not in a McDonald's restaurant. You may hold my hand at Christopher and Seventh, but don't dare try at West Third and Sixth. You can be my lover at my home number, but you will wait for my line at work. It's all right to be a queen if you want to be, but don't even think to be my friend. And the list of self-limitation and auto-repression goes on. The slamming of closet doors. Unlike when we were children, though, nowadays most of us learn nothing new about ourselves in these spaces.

The number of us who have recognized the trap that society has set for us, analyzed the treadmill on which nurturing has placed us, and who have escaped are few, and many of them are dead. Most of the rest of us are caught somewhere in denial, not realizing that the things we do—seedy or not—are not wrong unless they are terminal. If we disregard the fact that where we are today is a direct result of where we were yesterday, we will never be empowered to decide where we will be tomorrow. The counter to homophobia is not to recruit more homosexuals and to build more closets, but to abandon the concept of places and ways in which we are acceptable. Coming out is a communal concept that perhaps should be looked upon as "breaking out." Shattering the walls, the doors, and the hinges. If we cannot accept ourselves and do not embrace our own, we will stifle in our closets, and be discovered there dead.

NOTE

1.   Ki-ki: a term used by young gay men to describe a close friend.

KISSING COUSIN

by R. Leigh (Tré) Johnson

In the late 1970s, the city of Atlanta, Georgia, was in a state of emergency. A string of senseless child murders occurred. First, two little girls from regional area housing projects were taken, molested, and finally killed and dumped at area shopping centers and parks. Next came the little boys. Every day children ranging in age from seven to seventeen were snatched, raped, and finally murdered. All twenty-three kids were named Atlanta's Missing and Murdered Children. I never will forget the local TV station's announcement every night: "It's eleven o'clock. There's a curfew in Atlanta. Do you know where your children are?" I was seven and a half years old, a black male, and absolutely petrified. I was so frightened I couldn't eat, sleep, or go to school. I just knew whoever was responsible for these heinous crimes was after me. It got so bad that my parents sent me to Richmond, Virginia, to live with my aunt for my own safety and for my own sanity. The killings went on for more than two years. I called home one day to see how everyone was doing. My mother nearly broke my heart when she informed me that my best friend, who lived next door, was now a part of this dreadful list. It seemed I was now destined to spend the rest of my life in Richmond, away from all the other people I loved.

During the summer of 1980, Wayne Williams was convicted of committing two of the murders. The killings ceased and, with sadness, I returned to my native Georgia. I was now ten years old. By this time, my parents' marriage of nineteen years was on its last leg. My mother and I moved in with my grandmother and the most beautiful black boy I had ever seen, my cousin Somba (pronounced Som-bay). It was love at first sight. He was two years older than me. Somba was also curious and going through puberty. He became my first lover, which began out of innocence. The more we bathed together, the more we took notice of each other's bodies.

After a few months, our curiosity took on more "physically wholesome" characteristics. On a regular basis Somba would take every opportunity to piss me off so I would hit him. This would ultimately lead to a wrestling match in which I would always give in. He would hold both my arms down, look me straight in the eyes, and begin rubbing up and down on top of me, our bodies as close as the stars and sky. I will never forget the first time Somba had an orgasm. We went through our usual routine of wrestling. He jumped on top of me, and away we went. All of a sudden he asked me, "What's happening to me?" "I don't know," I replied. "What does it feel like?" "Like—like I'm warm all over, from my head down to my toes," he managed to utter as he panted. I thought, Hmmm. He has gorgeous feet. The more he hunched and grinned and squeezed me, the better I began to feel. Then he trembled and let out an enormous sigh of relief. The next thing I knew, there was this huge mass of slimy, warm, white thick stuff all over my legs and stomach. "What on earth is that, Somba?" "I don't know, Leigh. You did it." "No, I didn't. You did it," I responded with bewilderment. We both decided to stop "doing it" until we found out what "it" was.

A quick call to my aunt in Richmond set both our minds at ease. I explained to my cousin that "it" was semen and that it was used to fertilize an egg, which in turn makes a baby. And according to my aunt, all those feelings that go along with the process were natural because making a baby was the most natural thing that anyone could do. We resumed our curiosity again and again, hoping Somba wouldn't use up too much semen and then not have any left by the time he got married and wanted to start a family. Pretty soon the dry masturbation act was still fulfilling but boring. We were now ready to move on to the next level of our very active sex life.

It was the beginning of summer, my mother and my grandmother both were gone to work. My beautiful lover got up to
lock the door and resume the position of his powerful arms
pulling me closer to him. Each day my love for his arms grew
stronger and stronger. "Let's try something new, Leigh." Anything to please you, I thought. "What might you have in
mind?" I asked. "Do you know what a blowjob is?" he said.
"No." "Do you know what giving head is?" "What?" "Head?"
I had no earthly idea nor any burning desire to find out. Somba
explained to me what our older cousin, Dafus, had told him.
A blowjob was another form of sex. Only you use your mouth.
The more he talked, the more my stomach did somersaults,
cartwheels, and butterflies. "Will it hurt, Somba?" "I don't
know, Leigh, but you know I wouldn't do anything to hurt
you. I love you." That was all the reassurance I needed. So I
closed my eyes, said my prayers, and gave my first official
blowjob. The entire act took a total of one and a half minutes.
It was suffocating, nauseating, and completely depressing. It
was the longest one and a half minutes of my life. But Somba
was ecstatic. Again we met up with the slimy, warm, white,
thick, mucous blob. Only this time the experience was much
worse because I was also confronted with the displeasure of
its taste. I was absolutely sick. I ran to the bathroom and regur-
gitated, mostly due to that God-awful taste, and the minor fear
of a baby growing in my throat. Somba came to my aid a few
minutes later in the bathroom. "Are you okay?" I said nothing.
"I'm sorry." *Silence.* "I'm really sorry." My tears came down
like a waterfall. Somba helped me to our bed, turned on the
rotating fan, and put his strong consoling arms around me
with my back against his chest. The tears wouldn't stop coming. Somba remained with me the entire day just holding me
and wiping the tears away. I cried myself to sleep. We slept
the rest of the morning and half of the evening in the same
position until my grandmother came in from work. By this
time I had fully recovered from my hellacious morning. My
grandmother came in with her usual announcement and greet-
ing: "Hey, babies. What big mama's boys been doing?" Somba's reply was, "Boys will be boys." "And you, Leigh," she
added. My silence was deafening. My guilt was circling the

room like a vulture's descent on evening prey. "Nothing," was all that I could blurt out as an obvious blush of shame colored my face. She had to know I was lying. Later that night, before we went to bed, Somba came to me and told me we wouldn't do anything else until I was ready. "I don't know when that will be," I told him. "I'll be waiting. I'll be ready."

By the end of the week, I yearned for my lover; I needed his touch, his smell, his attention, his affection. I was again happy. To this day, I still haven't gotten use to the taste of semen, but for him I would have done anything.

My mother enlisted me in the neighborhood Boys Club for the summer. I hated that place. "Why do I have to go to that stupid club, Mama?" I asked on a regular basis. "You and Somba are too young to be staying here all day by yourselves. All day long you sit here doing nothing. An idle mind is the Devil's workshop" was all I got from her on that subject. "What can be so wrong with two boys, who are first cousins, spending the summer watching TV and playing?" I neglected to add having sex regularly. "What would you do if Somba wasn't here with you?" she asked me. "I guess I would have no other choice but to go to that dumb club."

I nearly fainted when Mother informed me that Somba would be going to Milwaukee, Wisconsin, to spend the remainder of the summer with his mother's people. My life was over. I cried every day, and I cried every night. I spent the rest of my miserable summer at Cooper Boys Club, totally unproductive and withdrawn. My heart was broken. The day before Somba left, we made a pact. "Do you promise to call me, Somba?" "They don't have a telephone." "Will you write me?" I fought back the tears long and hard. "If you stop crying, I will." "If I don't stop, will you stay?" "No, but I promise to write." He never wrote. For two months, not a word. All I could do was mark each day on my calendar, lay in our bed and watch for him in the sunset. That was the longest summer of my life. I felt that I couldn't go on living. It was as if I were being denied feelings and emotions that weren't sick, evil, or demented. I was in love, deeply in love. After endless nights of sleep and long days of anticipation, the Lord saw I couldn't be without Somba another moment. Another sun couldn't set unless I saw him.

Very late one night, I felt those familiar strong arms go around my waist. I felt the warmth of his black chest against my brown back. I smelled the sweet scent of Somba. A combination of Irish Spring soap and cocoa butter lotion. He was home, and I never wanted him to leave again. "We'll talk in the morning, Leigh," was all he said. "I love you, and I'm glad you're back." "Me, too." I slept like a newborn infant. I somehow persuaded my mother to let me stay home with Somba that day. I was eager to hear about his adventures in Wisconsin, what Milwaukee was like, what other people were like, why he didn't keep his promise to write.

As Somba spoke, I saw the transformation going on before my very eyes. He was no longer my "boyfriend/lover," he was now a man. I knew I was living on borrowed time. I knew very soon girls would start to appeal to him. I knew any day now all the things Somba and I did and shared would become "unspeakable." I knew this perfect love affair was ending.

Somba was now fourteen and I was twelve. We couldn't sleep together anymore. My parents' divorce was finally settled. My mother and I would be moving into our own place at the end of the month. I was now the one leaving. I can still remember that day, as though it were yesterday, when Somba and I "did it." Afterward, just as I had foreseen, Somba told me that it *was the last time.* He was now a man, having sex with the girl next door named Esia. As we lay there arm in arm, we talked of our prospective futures. He wanted to be a famous basketball player, and I wanted a career in entertainment. "I always want you to be a part of my life, Somba." "I will, Leigh, but not like this." "You've taught me a lot of things, Somba. I can't ever forget you." When my mother and I moved away, the good-bye wasn't as painful as I thought it would be. We were now our own persons. He had his life; I had mine.

For years the conversation, "Remember when we were children, how we use to play?" never came up. I later went on to become a singer and a writer in London, England. Somba left to join the United States Army basketball team in San Diego,

California. We both returned home to Georgia. "Somba, do you remember how we use to play when we were children?" We both laughed until we cried. I felt those familiar strong arms go around my waist, and I felt the warmth of his chest against my back.

LIKE THE WHITE GIRLS

by Tod A. Roulette

One of the strongest and happiest memories of my father is of the two of us riding bareback on the farm in Kansas. I was no more than four, but it is etched in the good part of my memory. I held on tight to his waist as the horse galloped across the pasture, my small, thin, tan fingers clutching around my father's dark middle, over uneven ground and tall grass. My eyes wold gape at the house, the VW and Ralph, the big German shepherd, as he barked and ran alongside us. And then my eyes would tightly close. Daddy was there. Later he would tell me that I wouldn't have to work. That, of course, was if his business did well. It did not, and he lost everything. But what I, a young and impressionable child, heard was: "Someone will be there to take care of you. Don't worry. There will always be a savior."

This is where I have begun to unravel the contempt, distrust, and ambivalent feelings I've exhibited toward many black men. I'm sure it began the first time my mother called the police when my father hit her. I was very young and don't remember the specifics. It's locked away somewhere in the part of my memory where bad things are tucked and hidden. Or was it after my parents' divorce when I experienced the ultimate betrayal for a five-year-old boy: desertion by his father.

Daddy got the idyllic farm; mom, sister, and I got some stocks and bonds, which were gone in no time. Business or another good-looking, long-haired, fair-skinned chick like my mother took priority over visiting or calling me. One day I sat down and reluctantly, amid tears, wrote him a letter telling him I never wanted to see him again. It was one of the first lessons I learned about remembering the good and bad and how to put everything I couldn't say or hadn't yet figured out in my head down on paper.

I was the only black in first through fourth grades. And I never really thought about it until there was mention in class of slavery or pictures shown of poor black people who lived in big cities. Then I felt all eyes boring holes through me.

We went to a black church, the only time I was around other black males my age. I admired them. They were cool like my father, so together and in-the-know. But they lived and breathed young, black, urban culture, and I instantly felt shut out. I spoke proper English with a soft, somewhat effeminate affectation, went out of my way to avoid confrontation, and never seemed quite sure of myself. I stood in stark contrast to the machismo, indifference, and detachment of the others. They didn't trust me nor I them. Before church I would be warned not to get into trouble with "those" boys. They were all branded hoodlums in my eyes. Just like my father. Although I don't ever remember anyone saying, "Don't end up like your father," the sentiment was all around. "Your father is a real slicker; he could con money out of the bank when honest people couldn't get money." "Your father threw pictures of you and your sister at your mother and said you weren't his." "Your mother should have never married your father." It didn't take long to figure out that I was not to emulate, aspire to, or even like my father. The men who took me to baseball practice, helped me earn Cub Scout badges, or took up for me whenever I was in trouble were the fathers of my white playmates. My father always had an excuse for his absence.

Then came Maurice—the beautiful, brown-skinned, almond-eyed, highly articulate new boy—to my mostly middle-class suburban school. Both of his parents were successful. No longer was I the exotic tan belle of the ball, and I hated it. I hated Maurice. Few got along with him. Nevertheless, I resented him for moving to my school in all his perfect A-plus glory. We avoided each other. He was as distrustful of me as I was of him, each of us pushing the other's buttons. Even then I was remotely aware of the complex psychological world we both had been placed in by our friends, our social class, white America, and our families. We were engaging in an on-going, unfriendly, unspoken variation of playing "the dozens," in which each vied for the attention of our white classmates, whose praise would validate one or the other of us, rendering the one not praised at the time invisible or unimportant. We were very black and didn't know it.

Not long after, I found myself at a new school, this time in the inner city. In geography and mind-set both schools were miles apart. The new school was almost half black, half white; half poor, half middle-class, with many fewer kind, polite people.

I was teased on a daily basis by mean black boys. And one day the harassment led to my being dragged from one street corner to the next by the same rough boys who called out the requisite slurs "faggot" and "sissy." It wasn't the epithets, the punch in the stomach, the blow to the head, the blood on my shirt, or even the humiliation of having a white woman jump out of her car to help me that really hurt. It was the fact that no matter how nice I was, I could never get in that exclusive black male bonding circle. Sure, I was taunted by white boys too for being effeminate, but we always seemed to make up afterward. It hurt, but not as much as it did when it came from boys my own color.

I was a small, polite boy who would curl up in front of the TV screen watching *The Young and the Restless* from the time my mother would allow me to touch the dial. I watched women being whisked away to marriages, large houses, and doting gorgeous white men, not unlike many of the women in my family.

At school, I always spent my recess with chatty white girls, swooning over the latest heartthrob whom I never remember being black. I knew my family genealogy pretty well for a fifth-grader. All those black/white liaisons and romances of my black relatives from the mid-1800s on must have meant something. My fate was sealed.

The black boys I knew may never have wanted my friendship, but I knew others who did: the white boys. I was always proud of my own male relatives: distant cousins, the uncle and grandfathers and great-uncles. I felt welcome there. I knew they could never kick me out of their clique. I irrefutably belonged. But there was this larger question of getting along and feeling comfortable outside my large extended family. The only choice I felt comfortable with was generally to steer clear of black boys.

My grandmother told me of one of our relatives who was passing as white and who occasionally visited secretly. He said, "You know I love you and all the family, but I just can't let my family know." Although the world he grew up in was more racist and segregated than the world I knew, I understood his reason all too well. Who needs the pain? It is the same fear of pain that I, who wasn't old enough to do long division yet, was so very aware of that I became enraged and ashamed that the gods had put Maurice and me together at the same school. I didn't want to be hurt. By what? Probably by being branded and forced to socialize with someone simply because we were of the same race. Afraid to be lumped together regardless of who we were. Maybe, more important, it was the pain and fear of my friends suddenly realizing that I was black, or, more fittingly, that I would realize I was black. Then all those ugly comments I heard from the time I was a small child—"Black people always have to go in herds, can't go anywhere by themselves," "They're always ready to blame white people," "They can't talk in a normal voice, always got to be loud like monkeys in a cage"—would ultimately indict me as well.

They swirled in my head like a turbulent tornado every time I wanted to assert myself, be loud, or be attracted to all those bad-ass "niggas" or to use the term "black." In my family "colored" was the preferred term. All I wanted to be was liked. Today I understand how even Maurice's benign and even very correct presence caused me such intense anguish early on; fac-

ing another black male brought my own displaced reality to a
screeching and jarring halt.

The late filmmaker Marlon Riggs said we are a people trying
hard to forget many, many years of horrors, injustice, and in-
dignities. It is amazing how the mind tries to heal itself. Sepa-
rating the good from the bad. One part goes here. Another
there. Double-souled paranoia.

After dating for the first time a black man, during my fresh-
man year of college, I panicked. Did I commit social suicide?
Would I ever get a date with another white guy on campus?
In an already tight market, I certainly did not want to limit my
options. I would notice myself walking in with him uneasily at
times, imagining everyone seeing us as making a radical statement on that mostly lily-white campus. I am sure some did
read it as very radical.

There I was: the jovial, campy, sometimes snooty, best friend
of materialistic white girls, who rarely spoke of anything political, unless it was gay, white-bread politics, walking around
with a black guy on my arm! Other times, I would become
very defensive of this choice. Not unlike a relative of mine,
who had been engaged to a wealthy white man and abruptly
ended the relationship and fell in love with a very dark-
skinned black man from the South. She now cries racism all
the time and condemns mixed marriages. She is not quite comfortable in her newfound black skin. And I understand.

The white woman who jumped out of her car to save me
from further physical pain at the hands of other black boys
could not heal the emotional scars I carry to this day. No one,
not a doting, gorgeous white man or black man, not even my
father, can wake me up from the nightmare of internalized
racism that continues to haunt me. Only I can do that.

THE LETTER

by Donald Keith Jackson

"Part of my soul went with him."
—WINNIE MANDELA

Dear Joe,

Your mother asked me, "Did you know that my son was special?" When I told her, "Yes, yes, I knew your son was special," my answer brought back those wonderful days we spent
together while serving in Uncle Sam's military. Both of us were
young and vulnerable. I was stationed at Cherry Point Marine
Corps Air Station. You, a Navy hospitalman, were attached to
a Marine Corps unit at Camp Lejeune Marine Corps Base.

I remember the day that I received orders to report to the
3rd Marine Division, Okinawa, Japan. My heart was broken
thinking of how I was going to live so far away from you.
You were so reassuring to me. You told me that oceans and
mountains could never come between us. You told me that we
will always be together " 'til death do us part." Joe, do you
remember how much we laughed until we cried when only
one week after my news of leaving, you said that your unit,
the 2nd Marine Amphibious Unit, was to leave for six months'
duty as a peacekeeping force in Beirut?

We spent our remaining days preparing to say good-bye.
This was going to be the first time that we would be so far
apart from each other. I was trying to be a brave Marine, but
baby, my heart was breaking inside. We laughed a lot and
talked a lot, sharing the things we feared. I remember your

83

face when you asked me if I really loved you. No, I said, I'm very much "in love" with you. I knew at that moment our dream of building our lives together would come true. We gave each other an early Happy Birthday. I was to soon turn twenty-one. We took great pleasure in preparing our last dinner together. That night we had veal parmigiana with linguine, a salad, and red wine. So many times while we ate, I would stop to watch you twirling the noodles on your plate. It was then I realized that our stomachs were full of butterflies, not food. So powerful were your touch, your smell. Your soft lips gave passionate kisses. And those beautiful "life-giving" eyes, all played a part in the intense lovemaking rituals we shared before we said our good-byes.

Arriving in Okinawa was an exciting and very lonely experience, especially today, my birthday. Twenty-one is the age when one becomes an adult, but today I feel like a little boy. I wish that you were here with me to tell me that everything will be all right.

Many letters and cards have been exchanged between us. Today I felt a strong need to pull out the first letter you sent to me telling me of your arrival in Beirut. You said that this is not a place to spend a vacation! It's the kind of place that could drive you to extreme boredom. I do not want you to be bored, my love, so I will be sending you plenty of letters and cards with goodies to keep you going on and going strong. We continue to tell each other of our lives in foreign lands. The one thing that keeps my sanity is the thought that our eyes will soon meet again; to hold you and to be held by you. I always think of your beautiful smile, the smile that could always penetrate me and give me a warm and secure feeling.

Another letter arrived today from you to tell me that the weather is "hot as hell!" and that you have been stuck with "duty" again. It was food for my soul to read that you miss me and you "love (me) so much." You tell that you received my cards and that it brightened up your day very much. Each day I live, I am living for you and me.

As the months pass, time is growing closer to when we return to the States. The letter that I received today brings me the news that during the middle of a volleyball game, your unit was hit real bad by incoming mortar rounds from the Drews and that you were forced to stay in the bunkers until morning. "Don, two Marines were killed, seven Marines were seriously injured." I hear the fear and hurt in the words. "It's so hard to believe it happened," you tell me. "Muffled and confused" were the words you used to tell me of how your days have become. "I wonder if it will end soon?" I begin to feel the tears rolling down my cheeks. Joe, I am afraid for you. As I begin to fold the letter to put back into the envelope, I say to myself that this madness will end soon.

Each night, I pray to God, asking Him to protect you from all harm and to give you enough peace of mind to maintain your sanity. I always end my prayer by saying, "God, I love him so much, please bring him back to me safely."

Tonight, I am going to take a break from writing and go into town with a few fellow Marines. I feel justified in getting drunk. Even when I was in town hanging out, I longed for you to be beside me. How much I would give to hear you laughing with me right now.

When we returned back to our barracks, I reached over the lamp to turn on the television in my room, not to watch it but to have some noise as a distraction. There was a news announcement that flashed over the TV screen, saying that there had been a bombing at the Marine barracks in Beirut. As I was trying to make sense of the message in my drunkenness, I heard a Marine shout in the background, "Oh hell, we finally going to go to war now! Better get your M-16s ready!" Honey, it did not dawn on me in that moment that it could have been your unit that had been bombed. I went to sleep.

After a long day at the office, I walked over to the Post Exchange to buy you a card. As soon as I left the post office, I walked over to the chow hall to grab a bite to eat. On the way, I picked up a copy of the base newspaper to read while I ate. Flipping through the paper in a very nonchalant manner, I came upon an article on the Marine unit bombing. A strange feeling came over me as I continued to read this article. Something sounded familiar, but I didn't know what. That's it! It finally hit me—this was Joe's unit. I almost lost every bite of food I had consumed. My heart pounded like a hammer. I rushed to my room to get a letter to match the address. I was hoping and praying that I was wrong. I stood in the middle of the room, trembling with fear because the letter in my hand matched the unit identification in the newspaper.

Before the sun had set that day, I had placed at least ten pieces of mail in the mailbox, each addressed to you. Words full of support and deep concern. Things were not moving fast enough. The mail is just sitting there in the bottom of the mailbox. Doesn't the postman know that I need to get these letters to the man I love without delay? Before I go to sleep I will write to you once more and say a special prayer for you, for us. I will have to be patient. I know that I must stay strong in order to survive, but I am getting depressed. Please, Joe, hurry and send me a reply, just to let me know that you are all right.

Weeks have passed, and it is now November. It's a Saturday and the mailroom is open. I remember very clearly the three pieces of mail I received: a renewal notice from *Ebony* magazine (I have never been a subscriber to it), a letter from my mother (I know that she is going to lay me out for not writing to her in such a long time. She would not want to understand that I have been a mess worrying about the man I love), and the last envelope, which had my address on the front. My heart skipped a thousand beats when I realized that the handwriting on the letter was yours! Quickly I went to my room to read the letter. Thank you, dear Lord, for not letting me down. You really heard my prayers. As I read each line of your letter, I could hear the sound of your voice. In its pages, you congratulated me on becoming a noncommissioned officer and told me that you enjoyed the Halloween card I sent you. Finally, I can sleep knowing that you are all right.

I don't remember how many times I read the letter. It did not matter, you were fine and that was everything to me. As I was beginning to put your letter away, a voice inside my head said, "Look at the postmark on the letter." At first I resisted; then I turned the envelope over. The postmark said October 20, 1983. My heart sank deep within me. That was the moment I knew you had died in that bombing. I knew that I did not have anything to give me a sense of hope that you were alive. I remembered that the bombing took place on October 23, 1983.

I was so empty inside, I could not shed another tear. All I could do was moan. Grieving widows and fellow Marines got sympathy, grieving homosexuals like me get interrogated by the Naval Investigative Services and discharged. I told my fellow Marines, mainly those who could tell that I had been shaken up, that my girlfriend had just been killed in a car accident. You better believe that when I told my story, I would be monitoring every word that comes from my mouth, making sure I used the "proper" pronouns.

How can I ever know what happened to you on that horrible night when the angels of death came knocking on your door? Sometimes when I think about your dying in those barracks, so far away from home, family, and me, another part of my spirit died. Joe, were you sleeping when that bomb exploded? Were you having a late-night conversation with another service member about coming home? Were you writing those wonderful words of love to me? My prayer will always be that you were in a deep sleep and felt nothing. I will always believe that.

They say that time heals all wounds. This is not a wound, this is my heart, a heart that was so full of young, passionate, and innocent love, now shattered. I feel so alone in my darkness; not enough light to guide me through this maze of misery. It has been so hard for me to come to terms with your untimely death. You were my first love. I felt that I could face anything the world put before me. Your love gave me courage. Only you and the Lord above knew the depths of my love for you.

So when your mother asked me if I knew you were special, I could emphatically say yes because your presence gave joy to those around you and most of all, brought to me the gift of love.

> Love always,
> Don

LOOKING FOR LOVE

by Jalal

Dear Brothers,

I recently attended a special service celebrating Valentine's Day at Inner Light Unity Fellowship, a black gay/lesbian church. At the end of the service, our pastor, the Rev. Rainey Cheeks, asked if any couples or persons currently in a relationship wanted to come forward and be blessed. Out of forty people present, one couple approached the pastor. After blessing this couple, the pastor assured the congregation that there were many couples in the black gay/lesbian community. The sadness in our silence spoke for us.

As I watched the couple being blessed, I gently rubbed a suspicious-looking lesion located near my left wrist. I was afraid I might have Kaposi's sarcoma. My doctor told me the lesion doesn't appear to be KS, but he will look at it again in three months. I am reminded of my friend Derrick, who at twenty-seven is dying of AIDS-related complications. I pray Derrick didn't compromise his health against his better judgment the way I did to please my partner. I had told myself that since my partner and I were both HIV-challenged, it would be all right if we didn't practice safer sex. The purple and brown spots that now populate my skin tell me I may have squandered precious seconds, hours, days, months, maybe years of my life. The men who pursued Derrick while he was healthy don't visit, call, or write him. Support group members and friends hold his hand. I wonder if any of Derrick's former lovers are wondering who will hold their hand as they run from him and from themselves. Not only does the fear that I might die lonely and alone often leave me frightened and depressed, it has also forced me to ask myself what experiences have I had to make me believe that I have ever been loved or am worthy of being loved by another black man.

When my last relationship ended, my self-esteem was as flat as an airless inflatable doll. I am the history his memory has folded and tucked away. This was my second relationship within the ten and a half years since my life has been challenged physically, emotionally, and spiritually by HIV disease. I tell myself that if black men are worth loving, somewhere in this city there is a man who won't need X-ray vision to see beyond my physical characteristics. He will know that I am not the sum total of body parts on a sex assembly line and will believe that black men are worth loving.

I grew up in a family in which no man ever told me that he loved me. My stepfather ignored me. My father's absence was as faithful as the arrival of *The Washington Post*. No letters or phone calls, just his silence which headlined the fact that in his eyes, I wasn't important enough to contact.

I learned to live with the shame my grandfather felt when he heard the neighbor's kids call me a sissy. The only time he ever touched me was to slap my face for "talking back." The rage released in that slap came from a man who could never slap or "talk back" to a white man and stay alive when he lived in Georgia. My grandfather and I rarely spoke to each other. His anger and silence taught me to keep my distance.

From books, TV, and conversations coming from the kitchen, I learned "nigger" was another word for a black man. According to the women in my family, my father was a "good-for-nothing nigger" who quit his job and moved rather than pay child support. I was his son, his namesake, who would some day be a black man. If my father was a "good-for-nothing nigger," then what was I? My stepfather was a "crazy nigger," who held my mother at gunpoint one day when I was twelve years old. Although my mother survived that day, I grew up afraid of black men. My father's absence, my grandfather's anger and silence, and my stepfather's violence, along with the racist expressions of hatred I heard from whites and the popular expressions of self-hatred I heard blacks repeat, all helped shape the image I saw in the mirror. I grew up afraid of the men I wanted to love me and learned to do without rather than ask for what I needed from them. No one handed me a map that would help me locate the love I needed, but I was determined to find it.

My loneliness often led me to bars. After a few drinks, I sometimes ended up in a nearby bookstore or bathhouse. What could I expect to find but sex and sweat while boxed in a peep-show booth or steam room with another lonely man? Some nights sex was all I wanted from another man. But there were far too many nights when I walked out of those closets within closets having left behind my sexual tension but not my loneliness.

The men I slept with during my early twenties could not afford to love me or be seen in public with me. When I was young, men stopped by at night long enough to have sex with my body. During this time, my sexual partners were either closeted gay or bisexual men who didn't take me to the movies, sit next to me on a bus, or speak to me on the streets while in the company of male friends, their wives, or girlfriends. Had I been a "straight-acting male," these men would have spoken to me. The pain I felt each time a sexual partner pretended that I didn't exist outside of my apartment was the price I paid for being fucked by so-called "real men."

I realize now just how unrealistic my romantic notions about love had been. In the past, I refused to have sex with gay-identified men because I thought that real men had sex with women. For several years I tried to find the better lover, the bigger dick, and the most masculine trick among the many one-night stands and brief affairs I had. Sex was my way of getting men to show me attention. At first, I saw nothing wrong with men calling me a "sweet bitch" and my asshole "boy pussy" during sex. But I wasn't a bitch, a boy, or a woman. I needed sex to be more than a dirty, shameful act. I wanted sex to take me beyond the distance a man's penis could travel. Very few of the men I had sex with held me or kissed me. These older men I was attracted to treated me like an object. Having sex with men who rarely showed me affection made me realize that I needed more. Prior to that, I had confused sexual intimacy with love. I was twenty-seven years old before I realized that I wanted a long-term monogamous relationship. Just when I finally began loving the black gay man inside of me, just when my relationships with black men began to improve, along with my self-esteem, I found out I had HIV disease.

After being diagnosed, I watched men who had approached me for sex walk out of bars with other men because I wouldn't sleep with them that night. Back then, I needed more than a night to feel comfortable enough to reveal my HIV antibody status.

It was 1989. I was living in a Midwestern city where very few men in the black community would talk about HIV, let alone date someone who was HIV-challenged. Six and a half years after the diagnosis, while living in Detroit, I met a black man I found attractive, who was healthy and who also had HIV. I thought I had found someone special. During our second date, he told me that he preferred younger, light-skinned men, but thought I was sexy, so he would try something new. I was numb. I felt ugly and insulted. He wasn't the first black man I'd met who put a premium on youth and light skin. He considered men with lighter skin attractive and men with darker skin sexy. Unfortunately, he wouldn't be the last man I met who wanted a trophy to validate his self-worth. I should have risen from my chair and walked out of his life. Seven months later I did, after failing to live up to his expectations.

I met my last lover at Dupont Circle in Washington, D.C., the day before the 1993 National Lesbian and Gay March on Washington. Two and a half months later, I moved to D.C. to live with him. Although he could be very affectionate behind closed doors, he could be equally distant when we were in public together. I was "a friend" when introduced to his friends and his "baby" in bed. He told me that he had never been in love before. Whenever I created a little distance between us, I was too far away. (Since I was his first lover ever to live with him, I decided to create enough distance to protect myself and to respect him.) However, when I drew near and tried to touch him, I was too close. Once, while dancing close to him in the middle of a crowded bar, he pushed me away from him. I was too shocked, hurt, and embarrassed to be angry. Sometimes, I didn't know whether I'd fallen in love with another black man afraid of emotional intimacy or someone with the heart and soul of a sociopath. Like my former lover in Detroit, he was ashamed of his black body. Whenever he held me in his arms, I felt he was trying to embrace his own estranged dark skin. Each time he pushed me away from him, in my heart I knew part of him was rejecting the image of the "nigger" he saw in his mirror each day.

Once again, I am confronted with many painful questions while standing naked in front of my own mirror. I watch the scars from old wounds turn bright red again. Did I need a man, any man, bad enough to set myself up to be hurt again? Why didn't I love myself enough to walk away sooner? My former lover in Detroit had been sexually abused as a child and refused to get psychotherapy. If he didn't love himself enough to get help, how could he love me? My former lover in D.C. was fourteen years old the day he decided to kill himself, but instead of taking his own life, he made a pact with his pain always to live alone. How could he love me? How could he love himself? Every time men like my last two lovers physically or emotionally pushed me away, I felt unlovable. Until now, I hadn't realized that each rejection transported me back to my childhood.

I do not want to give up on another black man or myself. Giving up on black men means giving in to the distance I feel when black men passing me on the street avoid eye contact or stare rather than speak. It means giving up the sense of outrage I feel at night when cab drivers refuse to pick me up. Giving up means giving in to the fear I sometimes feel when I hear the voices of black teenagers behind me. Giving up means giving in to the fear I see in the eyes of black and white, men and women, as I walk toward them after dark. It is the same fear my grandfather felt he had to instill in me in order for him to feel respected by me. Giving up on black men means giving in, once again, to the resentment that kept me from telling my grandfather that I loved him and would miss him while he was dying of lung cancer. When I was growing up, if any adult or animal had tried to harm me, my grandfather would have risked his life to protect me. If he had understood how much distance and damage was created by his anger and silence, he would have been more loving. I realize now that the men in my family and my past lovers were never the enemy.

After being HIV-challenged for ten and a half years, I am now finding love before my CD-4 cells run out like the sand in an hourglass. I don't want to go back to pity parties on bar stools and voyeurism in all-night bookstores. I don't want to rent any more hustlers who fuck me doggy-style so they won't have to look into my eyes or kiss me. I am learning that the more I love myself, the less desperate I am.

The inner voice I hear when I am alone tells me I am worth loving. No longer will I drown that inner voice with music, alcohol, or semen. My mouth and asshole are orifices, not door-ways to a dungeon. I will not give my next partner permission to hurt me. Being penetrated during sex does not mean I have to be passive or feel less than a man. I am having that longed-for love affair with myself at last. It means taking better care of my physical, emotional, and spiritual health. I will not allow any persons, fears, doubts, or diseases rob me of self-certitude. I know now that I will find a man emotionally healthy enough to love me. I won't find my soul mate while in the arms of a black man who still holds on to a Jim Crow dream: a dream that makes me separate and unequal—good enough to fuck, but too dark to love. Black men can find love in each other. Brothers, I challenge you to reclaim your power, self-love, and sexuality, and to find it in each other.

To all my brothers of African descent, I love you.

· III ·

FACING THE AIDS CRISIS

BREAKING SILENCE IN THE MIDDLE
OF A HOLOCAUST

by Rodney McCoy, Jr.

If you were living in the middle of a holocaust, what would you do? This question crossed my mind on World AIDS Day a few years ago as I stood in the subway station waiting for the train to take me to work. My neighbors walked about preoccupied with the business of their daily lives. My thought was that most people in this city live this way, "business as usual."

That phrase, "business as usual," takes on a horrible irony when one knows that African Americans are living in the middle of a holocaust. By *holocaust*, I am referring to its literal translation of "total destruction by fire." For black Americans, the fire is AIDS, and it is steadily destroying our community. We no longer have the luxury of regarding the HIV/AIDS epidemic as the "gay white men's disease." The reality is that from its beginning, AIDS has always been a disease that's affected us. As we discover how AIDS has done a number (literally and figuratively) on our community, I want to examine what I believe to be the main culprit: silence.

Looking at the impact of AIDS on the black community, it may be justified to blame the white media, the white medical establishment, and even white politicians. Perhaps a more painful—and more honest—assessment should focus on the many silences that the African-American community continues to engage in regarding AIDS.

Many of us in the black community still perceive AIDS as "the disease of the Other": faggots, homos, skeezers, sluts, junkies, to use more familiar terms. The "Other" mentality also surfaces when AIDS becomes "someone else's problem." The result is that AIDS becomes (wrongly) perceived as a distant reality.

Another silence we engage in is with death and dying. Since AIDS is currently a fatal disease with no cure, it becomes a topic less embraced by the community. There is also the unwillingness to deal with AIDS because of the related drug use and addiction issues. Certain religious beliefs and perceptions about the AIDS crisis stand in the way of effective dialogue on prevention.

The biggest silence is the one around sexuality. As an HIV health educator, I have caused groups of teenagers, professionals, parents, and elders to erupt into nervous laughter or indignant shock when I talked about fucking, sucking, blowjobs, eating out, knocking boots, fingerpopping, getting some, getting done, or doing it. I've been given a stare of utter horror when I suggest to certain individuals that they give condoms or dental dams to their friends or family. I have also been told by more than one institution not to give condoms and dental dams to teenagers.

Such reticence is almost laughable considering the popularity of certain television shows and recording artists through whom sex becomes an open part of our culture. African Americans, however, become the butt of the joke when we see how AIDS has posed serious health threats to our personal lives, our families, and our circles of friends as well as to our community at large. Given the recent revelations from basketball icon Earvin "Magic" Johnson, tennis legend Arthur Ashe, and rap artist/producer Eric "Easy-E" Wright of their HIV infections (and for Ashe and Wright, their subsequent deaths), AIDS is becoming a reality that is increasingly hard to ignore.

Writing this essay as an openly gay African-American health educator shatters the myth that gay and bisexual men don't exist in the black community. It also challenges the other myth that black gay and bisexual men do not serve as positive role models. Yet many of my brothers pay a heavy price for accepting these myths and functioning within a community that does not affirm and support our need to live healthy and productive lives. The price is a loss of self-esteem and self-love.

This lack of support and self-love makes AIDS a particular threat to black gay and bisexual men. With AIDS initially perceived as a "gay disease," many men who are closeted about their sexuality do not access the information necessary for HIV prevention. This lack of access is also true for many black men who engage in sexual activity with other men but do not identify themselves as gay or bisexual. Their inability to accept their sexuality may cause many men to experience drinking and/or drug addiction problems. Since drugs and alcohol lower the immune system and impair judgment, they pose a double threat of HIV infection to the men already struggling with issues of identity, addiction, and acceptance. Without frank discussion about what black men do together sexually, many of these men won't receive the support needed to maintain safer-sex practices, thus increasing the number of HIV infections.

The consequences don't stay with black gay and bisexual men alone. As the black community engages in dialogue on the survival of the black family, we need to consider the "disappearing father": black gay and bisexual men who die while taking care of their children. Consider the loss of this same man to his parents, his siblings, his lover, his family. Many professions are also facing devastating losses. Writers and visual artists ask each other who will fill the shoes of those making their transitions. Ministers see their congregations and colleagues of the pulpit diminish right before their eyes. Politicians, doctors, businessmen, and laborers suffer silently with AIDS while often mouthing homophobic statements and creating biased policies geared toward aggravating the situation, not solving the problem.

Lesbian-feminist-poet-mother-warrior Audre Lorde never accepted a "business as usual" stance toward her work as an activist. In one of her poems, she warns us against complacency and complicity with her statement, "Your silence will not protect you." Years of silence has not protected the black community from AIDS; it has made us easy targets. We must speak honestly about who we are and what we do sexually. We must lose the awkwardness and discomfort surrounding our discussions on sexuality. We must embrace the HIV-infected as we would those having any other illness, with love. As African Americans, we must understand and live the Ethiopian proverb, "He who conceals his disease cannot expect to be cured."

THE OTHER ORPHANS

by Robert E. Penn

In 1985, I had a very unexpected experience brought on by a congenital condition: an irregular heartbeat. My heart started to beat so quickly at the gym during a workout with my thunder-thighed trainer that I became dizzy and very angry that the pulse meter was malfunctioning. The trainer took my pulse and made me stop exercising. My regular doctor sent me to see a cardiologist. The specialist gave me stress tests and more tests and transferred me to a well-equipped cardiac care hospital ward. While there I roomed with Joe, an orthodox Jew, some twenty years my senior. It was one of those years when Easter and Passover occur during the same weekend.

In the morning hours, Joe and I pulled the curtain between our beds so that he could say his Hebrew prayers and I could sit quietly and wait for the awareness of God's presence to fill me. During meals and throughout much of the daily medical routine, Joe and I talked. He felt pretty confident that the doctors were doing their best.

I met Marcia, Joe's wife, on Good Friday 1985, just before Passover, and she was hoping against hope that they could be together before that holy day. In their thirty years of Bronx immigrant/Holocaust survivor neighborhood friendship, courtship, and marriage, they had never observed Passover without each other.

Marcia was very worried. Waiting in near silence for Joe to return from his graduated electrical stimulation, she moaned that she no longer knew what life meant. Her place in life had changed. She felt hopeless, unable to help Joe. And she asked me not to tell Joe about her fear.

I didn't need to. Joe had already told me that Marcia was taking his illness more poorly than he was, that she was alone without him, and he wanted her to feel free of the need to care for him.

After I was discharged on a suitable medication with no side effects, except depletion of my bank account, I stayed in touch with Joe. First, I called him at the hospital. Then I called him at home. He was not doing well, but he was in good cheer. We both thanked each other for sharing our faiths: I told him about my Quaker silence and he encouraged me to read *Pirke Avoth, Sayings of the Fathers.*

When I called a month later, Marcia told me that Joe had died. I sent condolences. I called again. Marcia asked why I was calling. I told her because I liked Joe very much. He had shared a really difficult time in the hospital with me, he seemed like a really good guy and that was very important to me because we might never have met had it not been for the fact that each of us had a similar birth defect. Also, "Isn't that what it's all about?" I asked. "Life, I mean. Isn't life all about people caring for one another?" Marcia tentatively agreed, surprised, I think, by my frankness and the simplicity of my words. She thanked me and added how lonely she felt and how tired and how much she wished she too had died. I knew she would never take her life, so I simply listened to her pain, loss, and grief.

Before meeting Marcia, I never thought about how difficult it is for the people who surround the sick. The sick accept the illness more quickly and seem to deal with it sooner. That's what Joe and I did. That's what some of my friends with AIDS have done. But survivors feel responsible. They are left without partners, parents, and children to love.

I have made many new friends as a result of the AIDS epidemic: brothers, sisters, fathers, friends, lovers, spouses, and especially the mothers of those who were dying, who have died of AIDS.

On the last Sunday of June 1991, right after marching in

New York City's Lesbian and Gay Pride Parade, my then lover and I visited John in the hospital. John's mother and one of his sisters were leaving as we entered.

In the twelve years that John and I were friends, I had often left telephone messages with his mother, since as a craftsman and performer with little disposable cash, John lived at home. But I had never met her.

I would always call John when I wanted to laugh. And within minutes of his first robust or later diminished hello, I would bellyache between discussions of Africa, sex, spirituality, theatre, music, fashion, people we knew, you name it! We laughed about it.

Since John's death on October 1, 1993, I often call his mother when I want to remember how easily I found humor with him. She too had laughed very easily with her talented, Afrocentric, African-Caribbean son. Sharing our memories of him brings back the joy he spread. As far as I know, John never officially told his mother that he was gay or that he had AIDS. Even though she and I knew very different facts about John, hearing each other recall his goodness facilitates the grieving.

We hear about the orphans, children left parentless as a result of their parents' deaths in peace and war, their parents' addictions, their parents' sexual orientations and choices. We hear about the innocent victims. And we hear that we are all affected by HIV.

Losses due to AIDS are rising by the minute. This invading alien affects humans regardless of sexual orientation, race, ethnicity, nationality, place of origin and/or residence, socioeconomic status, gender, or any other demographic factor. We are all under siege. And we have weapons available to us such as risk education related to the means of transmission: cleaning injection needles after each use; practicing safer sex each and every time, except when *planning* to have a child; and when nursing babies, using breast milk only from HIV-negative mothers or an uninfected substitute.

HIV/AIDS ignorance has been replaced by limited knowledge. I think we still acknowledge only a bit of the impact of this epidemic. Those affected—the lovers, the partners, the spouses, the children—are often described as the care providers. Sometimes we hear about the impact of the disease on the economy. There are abundant discussions of its ramifications such as the projections of the future monetary value of work lost and the escalating cost of proper medical care. But there are other side effects we haven't even begun to recognize: other people who must deal, in whatever way possible, with post-traumatic stress resulting from the death of someone with AIDS. There are many survivors: friends, partners, relations, parents.

Parenting is motivated very often by some desire to be outlived. A child dying before a parent is so alien to our thinking that there is no English word for a parent who outlives the child, other than, perhaps, "reversed orphan."

Craig G. Harris, my friend, colleague, and mentor also died in 1991. His enthusiasm for black expression, gay expression, and black gay expression was great; his self-acceptance, the highest; his honesty to himself, so vast it motivated many people of color of all sexual orientations and gay and lesbian people of all colors to be themselves.

Craig's acceptance of his illness was so great that one day he came into my work cubicle, with its big windows into which workers across the street could easily stare, and pulled up his loose-fitting African pants legs to show me the very large Kaposi's sarcoma lesion encroaching on his groin. He had accepted his illness and was negotiating terms with his T-cells. His matter-of-factness forced me to accept the reality of his cancer, his shortness of breath, his tremulous voice of partially concealed anguish, his jubilation at minor triumphs throughout the day like getting to a doctor's appointment without losing bowel control or the use of his limbs.

I met Craig's father and mother when they visited the office about a year before he became ill. They seemed like nice people. I thought they were very courageous for coming to an openly gay organization. Their love for their son was very apparent. I thought how nice it would be for my mother to accept my gayness as much as Craig's mother accepted his.

After Craig died, I put together his memorial. A daunting

task under any circumstances, but especially in the case of Craig, who was so loved and so accepting of the love offered by so many. With the help of several other members of New York's gay and lesbian communities, I pulled together a commemorative testimonial video, poetry reading, and a screening of a video based on one of Craig's short stories. The program succeeded. Craig's mother attended, and we became friends after that.

I took to checking in on Mrs. Harris. I discussed Craig's writing with her. I encouraged her to have as much of his work published as possible. I submitted his work to various anthologies. She expressed astonishment that so many anthologies wanted Craig's work entitled "I'm Going Out Like a Fucking Meteor." She would never say the "F" word and didn't understand why Craig needed to use such a strong term, but trusted that Craig had a reason for his choice.

What has struck me most is her willingness to talk. Craig's mother feels his loss very much just because she loved him and doesn't understand why he died.

There are no services in place for orphans like her. She must devise her own system for reconciling the physical absence with the perpetual emotional presence of her beloved second son, Craig.

Mrs. Harris told me that she, a mature woman, a black woman, a sane woman, a God-fearing woman, was going into therapy. I congratulated her with the same enthusiasm I had seen shimmer in Craig's writing and presentations because black people of a certain age just don't go to therapy. People of some classes traditionally don't go to therapy. A lot of people, period, find the idea of going to a "head shrinker" repulsive. But Craig's mother decided, once again, to be an advocate and supporter of difference, even when she couldn't predict the outcome.

During his lifetime, Mrs. Harris had been Craig's number one cheerleader. In his death, she has become her own principal advocate, pioneering a path for other parent survivors.

I wonder how my mother will handle it if I die before her. I wonder how my sister will take it. When I told Mother that I am HIV-positive, she responded with fear that she might not be able to endure my dying since she had already gone through the long, painful process of my father's death from emphysema. My sister said, in sincere honesty, that she resented the possibility of my early death because it meant that in ten or twenty years, she would have to care for our mother without my help. I wish that I could give them the acceptance of my HIV that I have. But I can't. Just like Joe couldn't give his serenity to his wife, Marcia.

I wish there were a service for those living with the knowledge that I am infected with HIV just as there was post-test counseling for me; just as there is living-with-HIV group support for me. Just as there will be care-provider support for my lover/companion.

We don't have a word for parents who outlive their children, and so we haven't yet seriously thought of providing support for those who outlive children who die young.

We should.

Staying Healthy in the Age of AIDS

by *Arnold Jackson*

AIDS is one subject about which I have *no* ambivalence. It seems that many of my opinions about AIDS stray so far from mainstream thinking that they border on heresy. For that I am proud. My sexuality certainly veers from the mainstream, and for *that* I am proud. My ethnicity *definitely* veers from the mainstream, and for that I am proudest. I am black, gay, *and* HIV-positive.

Staying healthy in the age of AIDS, or getting back our health, is our birthright. One reason I preach this stuff so much is that I know I need to hear it for myself. I am not a "health nut" by any stretch of the imagination. If you looked up the word "health" in the dictionary, I guarantee you won't find my picture next to the word. But like many, I *do* have an idea of what it takes to maintain or reclaim good health. And the mainstream model we have been following to treat AIDS and HIV *is not* working. We don't need statistics from the Centers for Disease Control to verify that. All we need to do is just look around for our lovers, our brothers, our sisters, our friends, and our family members who aren't here anymore.

When it comes to AIDS, cancer, or any other life-threatening illness, I always say there are two types of people—those who want to be saved and those who want to save themselves. Those who want to save themselves often do; those who want to be saved often die. If you have AIDS, cancer, diabetes, or even sinusitis, you have a responsibility to find out more about your illness than your doctor knows. Unless, of course, you want to be saved. If we want to save ourselves, we've got to do our homework. If we let the teacher or the parent or the kid at the next desk do our homework for us, what do we learn? Chances are, not very much. It's the same with our health and our lives. If we let the doctor or the case manager or the media do our work for us, we are giving away our power. We are setting ourselves up to be the victims of propaganda, of dogma, of psychological warfare, the doctor's prescription pad. Indeed, victims of AIDS.

Despite what you might think, those in power, those who are calling the shots in the war against AIDS do not want to see an end to this disease. AIDS is a multibillion-dollar-a-year industry. Those with the virus are the consumers, while those making a living off of people with the virus are the producers of goods and services.

Cynical? Absolutely. A couple of hundred thousand deaths can do that to a person. Especially when many of these deaths could have been, *and others still can be,* avoided. But where there is AIDS, there is money to be made and reputations to protect.

No doctor, case manager, well-meaning AIDS buddy, or magic drug is going to save us from AIDS. So what else is left? As I see it, our salvation lies in our Higher Power's will for us and in ourselves. That is *it,* my friends.

Staying healthy in the age of AIDS is not an easy thing. The system dictates against it. As I said a moment ago, the system rests on our continuing to get sick and die. If AIDS went away, Dr. Robert Gallo would have to look for another virus to steal. Dr. Anthony Fauci would fade into obscurity. The major research centers and teaching hospitals would lose a lot of money. The drug companies' stocks would plummet. There'd be one less freak-of-the-week topic for Oprah, Ricki, Montel, and Geraldo to exploit.

People are dying from what we call AIDS mainly from three causes: chemical intoxication, severe malnutrition, and mental programming to die. If all these things were addressed, and even *partly* resolved, AIDS would go away.

Recovering addicts are a special breed of people. Many of them have spent years drinking alcohol or shooting, snorting, or piping cocaine. They make a commitment to detox them-selves from these harmful substances and regain a life of dig-nity and consciousness. Then, if they turn out to be HIV-positive, most intoxicate their bodies with AZT, ddI, ddC, and the like, on the advice of their doctors. The only difference is that these drugs are legal and the other ones are not. So it should come as no surprise to learn that a high percentage of those who died from AIDS were drugged to death in one way or another.

It is true that there's a lot we still don't know about AIDS. On the other hand, there's a lot that we do know. But despite the mysteries, there is no reason to abandon common sense. As long as people with HIV are constantly given immunosup-presive drugs like AZT to treat a myriad of symptoms, and as long as we continue to take them, we will not be restored to health. Our breathing will be maintained temporarily, but we will die. It's as simple as that. It's not a matter of if, but when. We must realize that sometimes taking absolutely nothing is better than taking poison. The body has an incredible desire to heal itself, but we don't give it a chance. Suppressing symp-toms does not equal restoration of health. The onus is on us, not our physicians (because despite their good intentions, that is not their training), to seek out ways to restore ourselves to health. The hundreds of thousands of AIDS deaths in this country should teach us something. They need not have died in vain.

So what do we need to do? What is our homework? I think we have to answer some basic questions: Do I want to live? How long do I want to live? What do I have to live for? Do I deserve to be here on the planet? Once we start to honestly answer these questions, we can then begin to do something that nobody else can do for us—save ourselves.

Since almost all modern disease, including AIDS, is chemi-cal-related in one way or another, it makes sense to reduce our exposure to chemicals. We need to question the "experts," including our physician, and do our own research. We need to trust our instincts. We need to put healthy foods and supple-ments into our bodies, and affirmative thoughts into our heads.

If we are gay, lesbian, bisexual, or transgendered, we need

to proclaim who we are. If we have HIV or AIDS, we need to tell somebody. Secrets kill, and closets suffocate.

Do I want to live? You'd better believe it. How long do I want to live? I want to live to be one hundred. What do I have to live for? To love, be loved, and hopefully make a difference in the world. Do I deserve to be on the planet? Damned right I do!

· IV ·
RACISM AND HOMOPHOBIA

DEAREST BROTHER SET

by Conrad R. Pegues

Dearest Brother Set,

I see you. I know you. I hear you. Deep down I feel you. But what do you know of me? I am your brother. I am black and just as beautiful as you. But do you really see me? That is certainly the question. The only difference between the two of us is who we share space with in the bedroom. It's the only thing we don't have in common. You sleep with women. I sleep with men.

I know you think I walk around switching my hips worse than any woman. You assume my wrist to be perpetually broken and that I just love to wear women's clothes and lure unsuspecting black men to their spiritual deaths like a Siren.

It's funny you should believe all of these things about me, Set. I find it funny that you can fall so easily for a stereotype of your black brothers. Yes, some black homosexual men do dress up as women. Some of us are "effeminate," according to your definition of the word. But femininity and masculinity are all too often relative to oppression of a person's androgynous soul, which is the place where character should supersede absolutes of male and female. Do you ever ask yourself what kind of person I am inside instead of trying to categorize me by whom I love or by a perceived "womanish" quality. Evidently, love as opposed to hate is not enough. Many black men have so-called feminine traits and qualities that include manicured fingernails, earrings, and various hairstyles. I figure

the penchant for a certain elegance in style comes from appre-
ciating ornamentation of the body over the vapid strictures of
male and female dress and behavior in our society. With all
the varying degrees of style black men have come to be known
for over the years, I'm still the problem in the community. My
style is too blatant a blend of male body with supposedly
"female" behavior. But isn't the problem really within you and
your perceptions, and not me? My presence makes you question your limited definitions of a man. I also make you wonder
whether or not you're just like me in spirit and may be living
a lie. If I trouble you, then shouldn't you be doing some intro-
spection of your own soul instead of attacking mine?

To help in your soul-searching, you should get to know
some of "those people" you evidently fear so much. You may
learn that we feel just like you do. We have hopes and dreams
just like you do. And we, with our black skin, have to fight
twice as hard to hope and dream because the ghosts that you
make us out to be are not supposed to exist and have needs.
No, we have to fight three times as hard because of sexual
preference. But you deny all of these things.

Black people, like yourself, think that we're a scourge on
the community when, in actuality, we can teach you a lesson
about holding so tight to masculine reality that your penises
become your center for emotional and psychological fulfillment. Our presence asks the question "Where is your heart?"
If you look inside and cannot find one, it is not our fault.
You should become angry at yourself and the forces that have
conspired historically to deny your natural ability to feel as a
human being should. You see, these "sissies," as you would
call them, are stronger than you are because they know what
they are inside and have the courage to tell the world in a
swish of the hips or in simply refusing to lie when a woman
wants a date. Their lives tell you no lies. Does yours, Set?

Every time you get up, just before dawn, and go to work
for eight hours, does your life ring with as much truth? I know
too many of you who work like a dog, pay the bills, spill seed
for children whom you hope to send to college, and yet you
feel cheated. Deep down inside you're unfulfilled, living out
all the expectations of a "man" in a society that despises your

color. You scent the bitterness against you riding the winds of the American Dream. You can barely obtain it, yet it becomes the seed of your aspirations and your evil. You want all the material gains of the American Dream and the kind of respect born of acquiring things that makes and defines a man in white America. The rest of the world is shut out of your heterosexist dream. You would be the center of your home in the suburbs, the wife, the children, the dog, and the two-car garage. Homosexuals would disturb your aspirations for godhood, which exists at the expense of the humanity and self-determination of others.

What are you really gaining, Set? You have to struggle harder to define yourself as a positive when the media reminds us every day that from young to old, we're dying of murder, suicide, and physical ailments at an alarming rate. Not only have our bodies turned on us in the midst of a violent system, it is a fact that we're turning on one another as well. To grasp someone else's dream too often means that you have to attack me. Is white America's dream really worth so much, Set? Is it humanizing enough for both of us?

What is it that causes black men not to see value in one another? Wars and murder, like leeches, always attach and suck life from the host full of self-hatred and illusions born of a false sense of place in the cosmic order. "Man" becomes the center of the universe with all the sexist and homophobic baggage society uses to bind black men to a limited sense of self. Black men rarely realize themselves as sentient beings with the ability to empathize with other human beings. To ally one's sense of self to violent traditions that don't allow for the basic human capacity for diversity and feeling is tragic and deadly. Diversity is the key to the black community's survival as varying realities converge in a system of checks and balances to maintain an equilibrium that absolute ideals of a man and woman would destroy.

When you see one of those "sissies," you just don't understand it. A man's got to be a man, you say, and should act like one. But what's a man anyway? In this country, all too often it is a human being who's locked too tightly into a gender role: one that denies him the right to feel, to admit love, even with a word, and that keeps him from saying he's sorry when he's wrong.

What's called a man in this country is one who lives hard, is constantly fighting for survival, and dies young trying to prove to the world that he can be the kind of man who fits the mythic ideals of manhood. You want to cast stones, Brother Set, when neither you nor those whom you despise are doing any better psychologically because we're both black. The "sissy" isn't a sissy after all. He's a human being without an institutionalized sense of place within the larger society like you. The sense of isolation and rejection we both experience because of race is compounded for black homosexuals when black heterosexuals exclude us because of sexual difference. Many times you're interacting with us and don't even know who we are.

Brother Set, I want to tell you about the others among black homosexuals; the ones whom you don't see locked into your stereotype. In actuality, we're the majority. We don't blatantly wear our sexual orientation in public for various reasons that range from fear to a desire to conform to accepted "masculine" behavior. Some of us don't give a damn about your judgments on our lifestyle, and others of us are like chameleons who prefer blending in with the heterosexual social environment. Not being "effeminate" is no easy solution to dealing with the problem of homophobia in the black community. Its resultant psychic trauma on the "masculine" black male homosexual leads to paranoia and guardedness.

Some of us try desperately to blend in until we overstate our so-called masculine traits by deepening our voices or pumping iron to throw off any possible scent of sexual difference. We make sure we do not look at other men in the locker room, even when they are talking to us. We stand before mirrors and watch how we walk to make sure there is not the slightest swagger in our stride. Some of us date women. When these women fall in love and find out the truth later, homosexuals become the enemy of love and family values. Homosexuals are not the enemy of the breakdown of community; homophobia is the culprit. When people are afraid of living out their particular truth, the emotional well-being of the community is always at risk. Homophobia breeds the living of lies, causing black women angrily to say that there are not enough "good" men around. The war of the sexes in the black community fuels a lack of trust in black men in general. No one stops to ask if the definition of a man is really viable if it allows black heterosexual men to be abusive and emotionally inaccessible and causes some black homosexual men to play with black women's emotions in their attempt to live by the accepted standards of male social behavior.

Set, when trying to live a lie about one's sexual preference, your feelings get so wrapped up in what you're doing to hide your true self from the public that you don't develop an authentic emotional life. You push your true feelings deeper and deeper down into some dark corner of your psyche where they'll spring forth violently one day in a fit of rage, turn into depression or mental illness that will steal away the vitality of life or maybe shorten one's life. So, Brother Set, some of us hide so that you don't quite see us for who and what we are. At the same time, you never realize that your friend, your son, your brother is a "sissy" too who needs your support. Regardless of whether or not we're homosexual, we're still black first and foremost to the world. Our struggles in the streets and on the job often come down to the same thing: skin color. It is more readily identifiable than sexual preference. But the addition to our pain, Brother Set, is that we're sexually different from you.

I'm often deeply disturbed by the idea that I might lose you if you ever found out about me. It is easy for people to say, "Well, you didn't need him anyway." Deep down you know you need the love and support of other black men like you need water and air. Is it wrong to want your love, Brother Set? I love your friendship, your ease, and the way that you take responsibility for your own in the community. Your strength is admirable, but I'm reluctant to tell you all of this to your face for fear that you'll find me out. The slightest show of our need for each other for survival's sake frightens me, too. It could be reason for you to call me out of my name and distrust me forever. Your distrust would be a sentence of exile that I don't think I could very well stand. If you reject me, whom else do I have to turn to at home? And home, a place to lick my wounds when the world has attacked me, is certainly where my heart always wants to be. But fear so often pushes me away. Your exaggerated machismo and homophobia instills the deepest fear with every interaction between us.

Brother Set, I hear your sermon on any Sunday morning. I see you in your black bow tie. I see you all neatly dressed, espousing the philosophy of the Honorable Elijah Muhammad. I hear you on the radio trying to amalgamate your strong oratory while reading the Koran, your voice riding the waves of the radio into my room. I hear you. I see you. But do you see me? Two religions, Christianity and Islam, not so different after all when it comes down to me. But neither of you wants to acknowledge me, and I practically fill your stadium seats and pews every time you lift up your voice. Devotion to the spiritual element of the black community is much more than a word with so many of my kind. It's a way of life. I sing to make both men and women cry and know how to "tear a church up" while crooning a tune. Too often I sit in silence in your midst while being publicly denigrated.

How I've longed for you, Brother Set, to acknowledge me in a positive way in one of your sermons or speeches. My heart has palpitated waiting in anguish to hear you, for once, acknowledge me as your brother, too. Instead, you choose to incite the congregation's laughter and scorn. You think your imitation of me as "effeminate" and womanlike are absolutely correct when only moments ago you cried when you heard me sing. You ask for a laugh at a high price, and in the end we all suffer. Family members take your word as law and ostracize other family members. Young black boys find it excusable before human and God to beat up other black boys who they suspect are homosexual. Black men fleeing any "feminine" emotional traits become hardened behind a facade of machismo through which no man or woman can hope to penetrate to nurture them or receive the same. Where the emotional life is starved, the conscience and respect for human life are lost because to respect life takes a certain level of empathy that becomes woman-identified and behavior unsuitable for a "man." Brother Set, you fail to realize how deeply intertwined our paths are. While you and your audience laugh as one at the jokes made about me, the whole of the black community will cry divided and guilty at funerals, court trials, and hospitals, and will wonder where we went wrong. And who is it now destroying the structures of the family—the truth of my life or the violence of your so-called holy words?

Look over your shoulder, Brother Set. Look out into your audience or congregation. We come to give you support, not attack you on the basis of white masculinist definitions of a man. What traditionally has been called a man has rarely been admirable. The same definitions of man that allowed white men to buy and sell other human beings without conscience now grants you the right to hold other black men psychically hostage because of sexual difference. If you're heterosexual, you're a man. But if you're homosexual, you're not. Have you stopped to question the origins of manhood as defined by this country's laws and attitudes? Ever since we've been in America, our bodies haven't been our own. Don't you remember, Brother Set? We've belonged to Master Auld, Master Thomas, Mistress Bruce, and the young mistress not yet out of her crib. A white infant, at times, has had rights to us that we couldn't claim. We've all descended from those black men and women subject to the injustice of not having self-determination. We, as men, have come from black men who were made to give the seed for children for a white owner's gain in capital. Our black penises were subject to the white mistress's will when she resented the high pedestal upon which her husband and family placed her. We couldn't say no to her because her word was law, life, and death. She could scream rape if caught, and we'd die a horrible death, our penises cut off and preserved like a pickle. If she became pregnant, we were sure to be killed, having stained her pure white womb with our black animal seed. Our babies were either smothered or sent away. This is the atrocity of not having the right to one's own body. In the face of such rights denied, cruelty and violence will prevail. Are you any different from our overseers and masters of old, Brother Set? No, the past all too often establishes itself as the core of present cruelties. When you degrade me for a laugh or parable, the evil of slavery has just put on blackface and wears your name, speaks black vernacular, and loves everyone in the community, but us.

Look around you, Brother Set. See us everywhere. Black homosexuals, without stories, nameless and faceless to you. We're sending our own and other people's children to school, we're ministers to many of the sisters' emotional needs, we're some of the most intelligent and creative people in the community in science, the arts, literature, and medicine.

I look in your brown eyes and black face trying to identify with you, and you fear my look as one of seduction. I find your strength admirable, but admiration does not necessarily mean that I want to go to bed with you. Why should I try to establish a relationship of intimacy with someone who is either emotionally unfit for a relationship or undesirous of being with me? Black homosexual men too often get the same treatment that the sisters get in trying to form relationships: coldness, hardness, physical and/or emotional violence, and the lack of trust.

There have been those times when I've tried to love you actively from the depths of my soul anyway. You need me, Brother Set, for a better definition of your own manhood, and I need you. We are reflections of each other's wholeness if we can only learn to see more clearly. We have gifts to offer each other that are naturally made out of the best of our particular expression of humanity. You don't want to believe it, but I see the truth come to light behind closed doors when you're lonely and just want to be free of all the demands of being a "man." Although you'd never voice what I am, I think you innately sense it most at these lonely times, the times of our solitude. You're just not certain what to do with what you sense. It's easier for you to identify me as a woman (thus objectifying me, too) to try to extract some affection and emotional salvation from the imprisonment of your gendered self. We clumsily try to save each other under cover of superficial conversation when the loneliness of the soul in the night screams bloody murder through your emotional awkwardness and mine, and judgment along with rationale is suspended by human need concentrated. I find myself simply wanting to hold you and let you know that to feel is all right, but my fear of your rejection builds up a high wall that I'm afraid to scale. So, too often, Brother Set, I watch you flee out the door and into a less-than-merciful night, drink yourself into oblivion, and start a fight to vent the anger which is the only thing you've been allowed to feel. I watch you from a distance feeling the unspoken need for male affection and affirmation palpitating expectantly between us like a singular, rushed heartbeat. What words do I use to draw your love and affection to me without engendering your hatred and distrust or that of your wives or girlfriends who see me as competition? It is then that I realize the tragedy of having no language to name what one black man can feel for another without the burden of homophobia and traditional gender roles becoming grounds for war between us. And so we walk away from each other with our need for the other's presence lingering on the air like the smell of expensive cologne; the scent is one not to be forgotten.

Black male homosexuals are seemingly forever veiling ourselves and our pain just like you, Brother Set. And I guess I should not be surprised at the times when you decide to engage the truth of my world and reveal to me just how fluid sexuality can be when our lives leave little room for lies and illusions about what is masculine and what is not. It is at those times when you need the understanding of another brother that you seek us out, looking for something in the darkness of our bedrooms, the back street two-hour motel, and the backseats of your cars, reminding me that there is no such thing as heterosexuality or homosexuality. There is only human sexuality shaped by the needs of the soul and less the traditions of the society. And that which is pushed down deepest in our souls will, some way or somehow, surface like the Furies and wreak emotional havoc first with the strain of living and thereafter with every unmentionable orgasm and ejaculation with and into the body of those whom James Baldwin called the "anonymous sex." As much as I hate allowing you to cannibalize my body and soul in the night, I am just as tossed and turned by the same waves that deny you your human self. I am the ghost of your days and the desire of your nights. The fact that even when you're with me you're not with me is forever my nightmare. I participate in your lie for a few hours and subject myself to your denial during the day if we should meet in public. People say it's a choice what I do. Denial of the truth creates its own tragedy. To tell my truth, Brother Set, is my way of reversing the tragedy of both our lives and provide healing for the black community as a whole.

But those of you, Brother Set, who don't seek us out in the night still cannibalize us as well. You simply say we remind you of a woman in the texture of our souls. You sit with us alone, in a quiet room, and often speak of the things that frighten you. The vocal tone is much softer than the deeper one you use around other black men, especially when you're "shuckin' and jivin'." Funny, how you hide your true emotional self, too. Your softness is such a welcome change. I'm not the only one keeping my true nature to myself, am I? But our quality times together are rare, aren't they? It's so much easier for you to lose yourself in the public lie of manhood than to acknowledge how much we really have in common as far as emotional needs are concerned.

Brother Set, your laughter, your many hues and physical features, your strength, your beauty born of resistance to a crushing oppression makes me tremble. Your love of God, traditional manhood, and the teachings of alienation make white racists' jobs so much easier. And when will you realize how much we are a part of each other? When we're both hanging from the same tree or our blood intermingles at its roots, castrated with the same knife?

Brother Set, don't ask me to become a heterosexual lie to you and abuse some woman's soul. All of us deserve better than to have to lie to one another. Don't ask me to become celibate against my will. Some heterosexual brothers are so confused that I heard one say that celibates cannot make a contribution to the community because they aren't producing children. Don't ask me for my soul and body. They are the nexus of my truth in this world full of lies and half-truths. The truth should be a bridge and not a minefield. My self does not belong to you. Rather, ask me for my gifts and contributions that reveal the beauty of our common survival and the vision I have for the future. When we realize the truth of who we are in our basic human need, we are truly liberated to love one another right and naturally.

Brother Set, I am black, I am homosexual, and I need you to love me. I need to love you. In the midst of our collective disaster in America, hear my call of love to bind us together, one to another and nevermore be apart.

Your brother,
Osiris

I PAY THE BLACK TAX

by Mark Haile

I have started crying again because someone else has started crying again. An African-American housewife clutching her daughter. A Korean American whose business went up in flames. Friends of a slain teenager. I view the images from the window of my bus. They flicker on television. They are projected on my eyelids when I try to sleep.

I have wondered recently if this gift of sensitivity, this by-product of being gay, is a burden that I would rather not have right now. As a black man, I have another heightened sensitivity. Vanessa Herron of *The Philadelphia Inquirer* attributed to Bryant Gumbel the label for my other sensitivity: the "Black Tax."

The Black Tax began long before the police beating of Rodney G. King and is levied by many, not just the Los Angeles Police Department. The Black Tax is having to assuage someone for the hundredth time, "I'm harmless, really I am. I'm not doing Angry Negro today." The Black Tax is the churning in my stomach that comes because I supposedly have the omnipotent ability to instill fear in others. Every black male pays the Black Tax every time he sees that equation cross a non-black's face. I have been secretly counting the days until I am so aged and infirm that I will no longer be subjected to it.

I cried along with the rest of Los Angeles at seeing our city go up in flames. I cried at each flinching blow delivered to our living rooms, at each new outburst of madness. I cried, too, at the stories of humanity shining through. I cried when the smoke made the air unbreathable, and I cried out of exhaustion for having to pay the Black Tax, knowing that this tariff would have to be borne by me and all black men long after the last embers from the fires this time were extinguished.

For me it started that Thursday morning, as the newscasts revealed that all hell was breaking loose, that the rage expressed on the evening of April 29 was only the beginning. I realized that I would have to get new earphones for my Walkman on my way to work in order to be able to keep up with the unfolding chaos. Since all the stores on Broadway were shuttered after the shooting spree of the night before, the nearest place to my home in Chinatown Heights to shop would be at Echo Park Avenue and Sunset Boulevard. Even on that morning of uncertainty, the heart of Echo Park appeared normal and untouched by what was taking place somewhere else, somewhere seemingly far, far away.

As I walked into the first shop I saw, the Asian owner looked up, startled to see me, he started shouting hysterically, "We closed! Closed!"

At first I was surprised. The door was wide open, the lights on, the OPEN sign displayed in the window. I could understand his fear, although it had crossed over into what I considered at the time to be irrational panic. I said, "Thank you," and purchased the earphones at another store on the same block.

On Monday evening, long after troops had arrived and "restored order," I again passed through Echo Park, and saw that plywood had been placed over shards of broken glass in the window of the Asian merchant's store. He had been looted, wiped out, while the second store I went to had not been touched. Did I feel vindicated, in that others in the neighborhood had obviously singled him out? No, somehow I felt partly responsible. Even if he was the only business in the neighborhood to be hit, even if the list of grievances against him went on forever, this was not justice.

The Black Tax makes me angry that the fire at Frederick's of Hollywood was more important than a hundred fires in South-Central. I beg to differ with newscaster Kelly Lange: the presence of National Guard troops on the city streets did not bring a "healing, calming effect." And as for Ms. Lange's sidekick, Harold, Sixth and Union is *not* Skid Row—at least it wasn't before the fires turned this bustling neighborhood into a scene from postwar Europe. Lange was right on, however, when she quoted the English newspaper that said, "Racism is as American as apple pie." I'm amazed that TV's talking heads could act so surprised at learning that the rest of the world knows what white America does not.

By the way, Melrose Avenue, I hear, got looted. I wonder, did even *one* black teenager work in any of those boutiques? Wasn't it cruel to taunt inner-city youth with such flagrant and constant displays of excessive materialism? Or just plain stupid to think that they, along with the rest of Los Angeles, would pass up the opportunity to get their hands on some of that shit for free? Hey, that's the American way. Just ask Stanford, Huntington, Crocker, Carnegie, Mellon.

At one point, I heard myself thinking, Back in the sixties, this is what we thought the revolution was going to look like when it started.

This wasn't the revolution, but ash was falling democratically over all of Los Angeles. We were all going to know tonight what life was like behind the Black Curtain. We were all living in South-Central now, with the same fear of both whizzing bullets and uniforms.

Explaining the secular history of curfew in Western society to my Asian coworker, I stumbled upon an awareness of how this culture has always been afraid of the dark. I catalogued reactions to my black face all weekend. There were stares, smiles both shy and forced, and those who simply looked away. The seat next to me on the bus went begging. I was acutely aware of each new human contact. I was also an unwilling accomplice to my own compulsive desire to study, to know for certain if the bigotry was in my imagination or was it for real? If Franklin Delano Roosevelt, our thirty-second president, was right that "The only thing we have to fear is fear itself," looking into the faces of a great many Angelenos, I knew there was definitely something for me to fear.

By Monday, things started to get back to normal—the kind of normal that worried me. The kind of normal in which President Bush felt comfortable blaming "social programs for the poor" for the riots.

For the first time in the four years I'd lived on my street, I met with some of my neighbors. As I chatted with one of them, a group of Chinese-American students scampered up the hill, and asked in a mixed chorus of shy and exuberant voices, "Won't you buy a candy bar to help the victims in South-Central?" So innocent were their faces, so sincere. The smiles of children that I see every day, that never flinch from fear at the sight of me. Children don't demand I pay the Black Tax. I turned my head and looked up the hill to hide the tears that began to well up in my eyes. They would have thought it odd, a grown man crying as he ate a candy bar.

CONFRONTING ADVERSITY

by Bruce Morrow

My life usually feels like I'm balancing on a thin wire strung across the city. Sometimes I can glide effortlessly, never aware of how thin the wire is. From Washington Heights, where I live, to Harlem to Morningside Heights, Greenwich Village, and SoHo. I pride myself on my mobility.

With little fear, I—a black gay male—take the A train by myself to 181st Street at any hour of the day or night. But I tell Roger, my boyfriend of five years, who is white, that he can do no such thing. Take a cab, if it's after midnight, I tell him, and I worry until I hear his key turn the first of three locks on our apartment door.

As for myself, I tend to confront adversity, real and potential, head-on. My face twists and contorts as I try to keep my balance on this high wire. On the A train, my face becomes a hardened scowl, my eyes thin slits as I read the morning paper. My look says, "Don't mess with me. I'm serious. I don't have time for you."

When I'm at work at a university law library, I never let demanding lawyers-to-be get to me. My body language says, "I'm too fierce for power games."

Late at night, waiting at the door of the Limelight or Crow Bar, I'm confident, almost arrogant. My chin rises higher to insure that my "class" is as "readable" as my race and sexual orientation. My attitude says, This here's a diva moment. Ain't no party started right without the likes of me. I'm on the guest list.

Then the wire trembles. The salesperson in the clothing

shop in SoHo—early twenties, white—is overly attentive, following me through the maze of aisles to the sales rack and the dressing room. "Just let me know if you need any help," she says. "How many items do we have now? Let's count and make sure." As if it mattered to me: I'm just checking sizes before heading down to Century 21.

It doesn't matter at all, I tell myself. And then I'm walking with my boyfriend past a bunch of black teenagers on West Third Street and they yell out to me, "You just trying to sound all white."

The hairs on the back of my neck rise, and my high wire feels like someone is strumming the National Anthem as played by Jimi Hendrix. Are they going to mess with us, bash us? My boyfriend doesn't even notice and keeps walking the twenty steps to the subway. I spin on my heels and say, "No one's ever told me I look white. Would you like to try that one out, too?" It's not quite a Snap! but I had to respond.

To say nothing would have denied not just my race but my life, my family, my grandmother who used to tell me, when I was six or seven and didn't really understand what she was saying, how pickin' cotton gave her arthritis in her knees, in her hips, in her thick knobby knuckles that didn't bend some days.

Another day, I'm leaving a Federal Express office when a young black woman whispers to a coworker, "What a waste!" And it saddens me to tears right there in Union Square because I know she's speaking not just of me, but of all black gay men. We're a waste, of no use to black women, of no use to the Negro race. And if we want to continue directing choirs and designing clothes and writing, we better conceal our sexual orientation and hide our loved ones in porn shops on Forty-second Street.

A good black man's hard to find because the ones out there are either gay or in jail! Isn't that the saying?

I check myself, make sure all the symbols are in place: pink triangle, cowrie-shell bracelet, rubber-and-chrome-studded ring. My footing falters, my arms jerk out perpendicular to my body to keep my balance. To keep from falling.

I head for the Lesbian and Gay Community Services Center on West Thirteenth Street. There's a writing workshop there called Other Countries: Black Gay Expression. It's not my nature to belong to groups, and I've already spent three years in a graduate writing program, so I ask myself why I'm bothering. Why do I need to meet a bunch of people because they're labeled like me: black, gay, writer?

In the hustling lobby of the Center, I ask the information desk clerk, a spiky-haired blond woman with multiple piercings, how to get to the workshop. She gives very clear but very complicated directions which I forget as soon as I take five steps. Luckily, there are a bunch of black gay men (I could tell) heading in what I think is the right direction. I follow.

Although I think it rude of me to eavesdrop, I listen to my tall black gay shepherds' conversation about trips to Bahia for the winter, about closing estates and going to court, appellant court or probate court, to finalize the closing; they talk about the cost of the cremation ($500 for the basic in-hospital death, $700 with urn) and how they're putting off an anxious landlord who wants to take possession of the decedent's apartment as soon as possible.

The matter-of-fact language used by these men makes me feel uneasy, naive: They talk of the business of death and dying with the same ease that someone speaks of vacation plans. A cruise to the Caribbean. Summer in P-town.

There are about ten people at the meeting, each a continuum of the possibilities of black and gay—high yellah to burnt black, effeminate to androgynous to butch, statuesque as Magic Johnson and waiflike as Spike Lee. In the discussion of the writing at hand, they talk with conviction and passion—for words, for art, and for life. They speak of words mimicking the sounds of drums, conjuring voodoo spirits, words rhyming in patterns like blues songs and elegies and sestinas.

I find myself reveling in their wisdom and generosity, their ability to see that life is infinitely more complex than any label or category—gay or straight, black or white, male or female. I think of my trembling high wire, of a white saleswoman, a black FedEx clerk. I think of my isolation. And it comes to me that the people in the workshop—like many others before them: Randall Kenan, Essex Hemphill, Samuel R. Delany, Assotto Saint, James Baldwin, Countee Cullen—are my safety net, ready to catch me if I should fall.

WHY I'M NOT MARCHING

by David Frechette

The white gay political party line for some time has been that homophobia is one of the major enemies of gay people. Homophobia may be a major concern for white gays, but for most black gay males—unless they're doctors, lawyers, or Harvard grads—racism is a far more formidable opponent.

Mention gay racism to most white gays and their eyes roll toward heaven as they attempt to stifle yawns. Complaints about gay racism fall on ears as deaf as those of a pharaoh of ancient Egypt. The only thing more boring, however, than hearing about incidents of gay racism is being victimized by them.

I can get into a "redneck" bar in Texas without incident—at least not until *after* I sit down. A few blocks away, though, at a gay bar or a Club Bodycenter, they'll insist that I cough up three pieces of photo ID, with my birthdate on them.

Hearing white gays compare black and gay oppression evokes a wide range of negative emotions from blacks, from mild irritation to total dismay. These comparisons become particularly odious when white gays utilize them to illustrate how their alienation from mainstream society has enabled them to "understand" the oppression of blacks. (If *only* this were true!)

Gay racism has many faces and, when you're black, they have a way of seeking you out.

At a Gay Press Association meeting I attended several years ago, one of its officers made the following statement: "According to statistics, blacks, although notoriously undereducated, have an inexplicable taste for high-priced liquor and Cadillacs." I pinched myself to make sure I wasn't imagining things. No one in the otherwise lily-white assemblage, which included representatives from such bastions of political correctness as Boston's *The Gay Community News*, bothered to challenge the remark: in fact, they acted as though nothing had happened. When I complained about the racist comment, I was told I was overreacting. Most white gays pretend that racism doesn't exist even as they practice it.

White gays carry on continuously about job discrimination, but how many gay businesses are actually equal opportunity employers? How often does one see gay businesses advertising in the Help Wanted columns? Many job opportunities are shared primarily among a close network of friends, and such networks seldom include blacks. Consciously or unconsciously, white gays often exhibit a deep concern for the economic survival of other white gays and little or none for minorities.

Most gay social groups have few black members and can't imagine why. Blacks often feel unwelcome or barely tolerated in many of these groups and fail to return after a few visits. Unless they're given by white gays with a "leftist" bent, white dances (and discos) exclusively play Eurodisco as though Whitney Houston and Aretha Franklin didn't exist. When you can hear more of a cultural cross section of music on television or at a Columbus, Ohio, senior prom than you can at your average gay dance, there's a problem. The problem won't go away by suggesting that blacks go somewhere else to dance, either.

Black gay men seeking acceptance into white social circles often feel compelled to file down their personalities to fit into narrow categories—intellectuals, studs, or carbon copies of whites themselves. For some of us, the need for acceptance within the mainstream community is great. *Essence* magazine once ran a display ad depicting a little girl looking at a display of women's magazines from which *Essence* was conspicuously absent. The copy read something to the effect of: Ever get the feeling when they talk about women, they're not talking about you? Among black gays that feeling of invisibility is common. Gay literature—books, newspapers, and magazines—as well as film and theatrical efforts either studiously ignore blacks or gratuitously insult them. Except for a small handful of works, films like *Word Is Out* and *My Beautiful Laundrette,* or books like Alan Ebert's *The Homosexuals,* gay has been synonymous with whiteness. All of this has a negative affect on the self-image of gays who are not white.

As a black gay writer, I often find it difficult to trust white gay editors. One editor told me how much he just *loved* a forthcoming piece of mine. When he finally published it, not only was it drastically cut, but all references to the black community, gay and straight, had been deleted. When I asked what happened to my story, I was met with a hostile response.

During the old Firehouse days of the Gay Activists Alliance in the 1970s, I asked a "radical" friend active in the gay political movement if the group had any plans to discuss gay racism. He said that it had been decided that gay racism would only "clutter up" the group's agenda. That was over a decade ago, and the agenda *still* hasn't cleared. Now the *New York Post* can be zapped for homophobia, but not for its lack of employment opportunities for minority journalists.

Homophobia is not something I take lightly—indeed, it hinders my dealings with several family members. But when I give my time and energy to an organization, I want something out of it as well. There's no point in me marching to benefit white gay issues when my own issues are either ignored or placed on a back burner with no pilot light. It is difficult, if not downright impossible, to build coalitions with people who don't take your problems as seriously as they do their own.

PROJECT ERASURE

by Fabian Thomas

With my curiosity piqued by the fact that my ex-lover was fulfilling his dream of becoming a New York City transit cop and that we had always argued about the closetedness of police life, I watched Phil Donahue's show on gay cops. I got a pleasant and unexpected surprise, Donahue did not annoy me. He wasn't trite, snide, or condescending. And he didn't show-boat or melodramatize. His guests were well-spoken, forthright, and actually included a lesbian. I was impressed.

Then came the questions from the studio audience, who made, for the most part, politically correct comments. There were, however, a few, as there always are, who wanted to know why these self-identified, out, and proud gay and lesbian cops couldn't stay in the closet and be happy they had jobs? Why was being *out* so important? One man self-righteously proclaimed that he doubted one guest's claims that his fellow officers and friends turned against him when they found out he was gay. "I'm sure we're missing a piece of the puzzle," he quipped. What an idiot! I thought. When was the last time you experienced racism, bigotry, or homophobia? Is your myopia so chronic that you don't realize that you don't have to do anything to be a target, except be or appear to be the *wrong* thing! As it went on, it struck me like a blow to the stomach that these smiling, indignant ignoramuses wanted me and my kind to be invisible, to disappear, to carry our closets like gay Atlases in some homophobic existential adage. I recognized that as long as we affirm ourselves as lesbians and gay men, people will try to erase us.

Understand clearly that this was not a new revelation. But each new reminder smarts and jabs at my spirit, further illustrating the cold reality that in this lavender life people will come for you. If you exist, they will come—for you, that is! Mother Maya Angelou calls them ducks. Ducks who will peck you to death. Steady, subtle, yet malicious pecking—taking the flander of your nose, your earlobe, gouging the nape of your neck—hoping you don't notice until it's too late. Not having the guts to kill you outright, they gnaw away at you surreptitiously.

Yes, they will come for you. Not just for what you have or own, for that is ephemeral and replaceable, but for your space, your life, your very soul—the essence of your personhood.

The gay basher is blatant and loathsomely honest. He or she comes to beat you down and kill you. This attempt at erasure is unequivocal. But the world is replete with deceptively civil homophobes who do not sport baseball bats and are often mistaken for friends. One can see a baseball bat coming and prepare a frantic plan of action, but what do you do with the concerned, incensed, puzzled, and TV talk showesque outpourings from friends, family, and neighbors? Those innocent comments that are really corrosive bullets of derision and erasure?

In the midst of these assaults, as I dream of an effective defense, I imagine this to be my mantra:

"Don't come for me! Don't come for my sisters and brothers. Don't come for our lovers or our children. That's right, I said don't come for me because I am NOT the one! You cannot have my space or my soul. You cannot make me invisible or erase me! You cannot make me straight or live in a closet. You can break my body, but you cannot negate my life and besides, I'm not alone. I've got family of the lavender persuasion everywhere. We are beautiful, fierce, and ubiquitous. Deal with it! And if you decide to come for me, you better have murder on your mind because I am ready

> to die. *And fuck that Phoenix or swan song shit! My orishas*
> *will extract a revenge that will detonate in your souls*
> *forever!"*

But as soon as I get myself worked up into a lather over
this, I think of how we, as lesbians and gay men, participate
in our erasure. We keep ourselves separate, attack one another,
negate one another's existence, and shorten our own lives. We
use the words "faggot," "queen," "drag queen," "sissy,"
"dyke," "bulldagger," and "fag hag" to address one another,
not with love or endearment, but in the derogatory way they
are used by heterosexists. We don't seem to realize that these
words drip with malice and poison that seep into our clothes,
hang heavy and malevolent in the air, and weave themselves
into the tapestry of our lives. As we wound and malign ourselves, we erase one another. We pose a threat to our own
existence. Don't we have enough shit in the world intent on
doing us in? Irony of ironies, in the race for our lives, we must
run against ourselves as well.

It seems that internalized homophobia, our own Project
Erasure, will get us if all else fails. That is, if we don't wake
up. We have to find the space, the guts, the audacity to love
one another, if we want to survive. I mean really nurture one
another, affirm our own lives. The travesty of sexual politics
is something we learned from heterosexuals and we need to
unlearn that shit real quick!

No, not all lesbians dress like men or have chronic penis
envy! Top and bottom are simply childish labels. Taking a
dick up your ass does not jeopardize your masculinity. "Drag
queen," "transvestite," "transsexual" are not synonyms. A
drag queen's life is valid by virtue of the fact that she is alive
and that she makes a political statement just by daring to put
on a dress. Who the hell do you think was at the helm of the
Stonewall riots in 1969?! And yes, transsexuals are human beings who deserve love and respect! If you have problems or
questions, ask for answers, read a book, or see a shrink, but
let's stop defiling our own nest, eating our young, reviling
ourselves, and negating who we are. For our own sakes, stop
participating in Project Erasure.

I dream of the day when we can love and affirm one another. I yearn for pictures of us holding and supporting one another—the boy who thinks he's butch; the bonafide banjee boy; the drag queen; the snap diva; the girl who used to be a boy and vice versa; the lesbian who is more man than me; the dyke who is more femme than my mother; gay parents and their children; those of us who are HIV-positive, symptomatic, asymptomatic, PWAs (people with AIDS); HIV-negative and those too scared to get tested; those of us who get high and those of us who don't; the ones who like it rough, gentle, on their knees, backs, bellies, indoors, outdoors, every day, weekly, monthly, annually; the celibate—all of us in all our colors, shades, shapes, sizes, religions, proclivities, and persuasions. All of us together, holding, hugging, touching, loving. If we could overcome the battle within, maybe we'd be able to heal the wounds inflicted from without by the hatemongers and band together in love to stop or hinder Project Erasure.

THE EMERGENCE OF AN AFRICAN
GAY AND LESBIAN COMMUNITY

by Cary Alan Johnson

Though rapidly changing in and of themselves, Western notions of homosexual "lifestyle" (exclusively same-sex object
choice, childlessness, emotional and financial distance from traditional family structures) can be viewed as conflictual with
traditional African values. In most precolonial African groups
reproductive fertility and responsibility to an extended family
were highly prized characteristics of both men and women.
Contrary to the ideals of individualism and personal rights
that have come to characterize Western society, an African
worldview tends to emphasize rights and duties equally.

> Asmarom Legesse claims that "no aspect of Western civiliza-
> tion makes an African more uncomfortable than the concept
> of the socialized individual whose private wars against soci-
> ety are celebrated." Benoit Ngom further contends that Afri-
> cans have no notion of private (individual) life; even
> lovemaking has a ritualized, public nature to it. Osusola Ojo
> agrees that "the Africans assume harmony, not divergence
> of interests . . . and are more inclined to think of their
> obligations to other members of society rather than their
> claims against them."[1]

African communalism however is not nearly as harmonious
a concept as these scholars argue. Individualism and personal

rights, including the right to protection from one's own group, are becoming increasingly valued in Africa and ingrained in national constitutions and regional human rights treaties.

The views of African leaders are slowly beginning to reflect changing attitudes toward homosexuality. The application for United Nations Economic and Social Committee (ECOSOC) consultative status submitted in 1991 by the International Lesbian and Gay Association, though unsuccessful at that time, was supported by delegates from both Ethiopia and Lesotho. The Ethiopian representative stated that "this is an example of the problems confronting minorities. The United Nations should be the last place to exercise discrimination." The representative from Lesotho went further, advising his colleagues that a positive vote was "a chance for us to liberate ourselves."[2] The African National Congress buoyed by the participation of gay and lesbian activists in the anti-apartheid struggle held fast to their commitment to legislation prohibiting discrimination on the grounds of sexual orientation in the constitution for a new South Africa.

Nevertheless, men and women known to engage in homosexual behavior face significant prejudice in Africa. Though increasingly visible in urban areas, those seeking to live outside of traditional roles face a variety of responses from their communities, including disbelief, ridicule, contempt, and sometimes police harassment. This discrimination, however, has seldom taken the form of long-term detention or torture the way it has in Latin America, Asia, or Central Europe.[3]

Despite the allegations of some African politicians that homosexuality is a purely Western phenomenon, most African nations have laws that prohibit sexual contact between men, statutes adopted mainly from the jurisprudence of their former colonial occupiers. The need for laws to regulate behaviors that do not exist has not yet been explained.

Homosexual men have been present as important actors in many African societies. It is only in modern history, however, and in urban settings that we can begin to identify a "gay" community by Western definitions. That is, the social networks, formal and informal, in which homosexual and bisexual men meet, entertain, seek and provide information and support, and enter into relationships with other men. Though these networks are often clandestine and virtually invisible to an outsider, they are fast becoming an undeniable element of urban African life.

Just as the development of gay and lesbian political organizations and social networks in the West has evolved over time, similar institutions are emerging with their own particular forms and styles in Africa. Traditional roles of all kinds are being questioned, discarded, and retooled in African cities throughout the continent. If the available historical literature is representative, we are beginning to experience more consensual age/status-equal sexual behavior between adult males.

Bars frequented by African male homo/bisexuals have existed for the last ten years in Abidjan, Dakar, Lagos, and Nairobi. In North Africa, *hammams* or bathhouses serve as meeting grounds for homosexual and bisexual men. Gay and lesbian organizations are currently functioning in Ghana, Zimbabwe, and South Africa. Liberia's gay organization had over seventy-five members prior to the recent political shredding in that country.[4] According to Nigeria's *Quality Magazine*, homosexuals

> are getting more and more aggressive and courageous by the day and are made up of the top brass in the society—successful lawyers, doctors, swanky businessmen, military men, ex-politicians, diplomats and university undergraduates, all with a passion for men.[5]

While this may be something of a paranoid response to the increased visibility of homosexually identified men in Africa, allegations of homosexuality were used against Nigerian head of state Ibrahim Babangida as an excuse for the staging of a military coup to unseat him, indicating the willingness of the Nigerian populace to acknowledge the existence of homosexuals within the highest ranks of their society.[6]

As in communities of color in the United States, the AIDS crisis in Africa has built a bridge between those known to engage in same-sex behavior and others who regularly engage in high-risk activities. AIDS prevention and support agencies are in general welcoming to gays and lesbians, both as clients and as volunteers, and have helped to diffuse the misunderstanding and contempt many members of the larger community feel toward homosexuals. These agencies and the social networks they create are likely to become the nuclei of more politicized homosexual organizations in the future.

The discussion of homosexuality in contemporary Africa would not be complete without reference to the influence of foreign gays, particularly Europeans and North Americans, who play a pivotal role in urban homosexual male subcultures. Unfettered by the traditional values and societal pressures that tend to silence Africans, the homes of Europeans become headquarters for homosexual nexus. Male prostitution emerged in African cities, as it did elsewhere in the developing world, to service the appetites of an expatriate homosexual elite and the burgeoning tourist trade. (See V. S. Naipaul's *In a Free State*, Spartacus's *Gay Guide to the World*.) Homosexual relationships between expatriates and Africans are also common, many having an informal financial component. White gays, be they missionaries, businessmen, or Peace Corps volunteers, have helped to disseminate Western concepts of homosexuality in Africa.

Still, homosexuality remains heavily stigmatized and Africans who engage in homosexual relationships lead secretive lives. Most are partners in heterosexual marriages, playing the roles African society demands of them, that of father and breadwinner, thus maintaining their community's (often feigned) ignorance of their homosexual activities.

According to one young activist,

Here in Ghana, Gay life is very hard. I mean since it is not legalized, all of our activities are behind closed doors. Though we are as many as one can imagine, each and every one of us is afraid to come out of his/her shells, be vocal. Besides the people take homosexuality as a taboo and therefore a disgrace to a family. Gays are absolutely neglected in the system. If one is found to be Gay, he can easily lose his job and at any social gatherings, he is neglected. But among ourselves, we are happy because though we are not legalized, we have free movement, by organizing parties, go to beaches

*and the like. (sic) But the next problem is how to get people
educated on the issue of homosexuality. . . .*[7]

African literature, while still maintaining a significant bias
against homosexuality, has at last started to include some homosexual characters. Novels such as Yulisa Amadu Maddy's
No Past, No Present, No Future, published by the prestigious
African Writers Series, and more recently Thomas Mpoyi Bua-
tu's *La Reproduction*, are paving the way for a new look at the
subject by African intellectuals and writers.

The evidence demonstrates that homosexuality is not new
to Africa, but is located within a rich tradition of accommoda-
tion to diversity. Through the institutions of boy wives, spirit
mediumship, and male initiation rituals, homosexuality was
indeed a regular part of the sexual patterns of many African
ethnic groups.

Why was homosexuality accepted in some cultures, but
marginalized or rejected in others? Given the integral role of
homosexuals in some African cultures, is there a corollary tolerance for urban gays in the cities to which such ethnic groups
migrated? If not, what are the roots of modern intolerance,
and how can it be combated? These and other questions are
raised for future scholarship.

There are two Akan maxims that seem relevant in conclud-
ing the very beginning of this important discussion that must
be taken up by other social scientists:

> *"Everyone is the offspring of God; no one the offspring of
> the earth." Everyone has the right to pursue their unique
> destiny and no one is a lesser person.*

> *"Nobody was there when I was taking my destiny from
> God." Despite the strong sense of African communalism,
> everyone has a right to privacy and to negotiate their own
> destiny within their moral conscience.*[8]

The moral basis for a gay rights movement in Africa is thus
already in place. It need only be further elaborated through an

open-minded examination of African attitudes toward diversity.

The historical basis is also available, but needs further unearthing by enlightened scholars, particularly Africans, who can dig through the cultural biases, their own and those of others, to amass a body of serious scholarship on homosexuality in Africa.

NOTES

1. Rhoda E. Howard, "Group Versus Individual Identity in the African Debate on Human Rights," *Human Rights in Africa*, ed. Abdullahi Ahmed An-Na'im and Francis Deng (Washington, D.C.: The Brookings Institution, 1990), p. 162.

2. Statements made at ECOSOC Non-Governmental Organizations Hearing, 22 January 1991.

3. Amnesty International, *Breaking the Silence*, AI Secretariat, February 1997.

4. L. McCauley, interview with author, 5 March 1991.

5. Robert Egbi, "Men with a Passion for Men," *Quality*, 16 June 1988, p. 10.

6. "Successful Coup Announced," *FBIS*, 23 April 1990, p. 20.

7. Anon, letter to author, 1 November 1990.

8. Kwasi Wiredu, "An Akan Perspective on Human Rights," *Human Rights in Africa*, ed. Abdullahi Ahmed An-Na'im and Francis Deng (Washington, D.C.: The Brookings Institution, 1990), pp. 244–45.

SOME OF MY WORDS

by Lawrence Dewyatt Abrams

Sometimes I wake up in the middle of the night, running from dreams polluted with reddened headlines with black faces. Once upon a time, I used to suffer alone; now, I roll over and cling to my lover—my double brother—and I find solace from the passing storm in his arms. I remember that as a child I found comfort in my mother's bosom and in my prayers to a Christian version of a Creative Force. However, as a black child learning to love men in America, the innocence of childhood was lost very early. And soon I found myself able to find comfort only with my pen, my man, and a few similarly endangered friends.

Together we teeter on the edge of society holding one another up as we fight to maintain our own stability. We each use our special talents to buffer the oppressive damage done to our individual psyche and our collective wisdom. Some of us are singers. Some of us are snap queens. Some of us are dancers. I'm a writer, both cursed and blessed with my ability to chronicle the lives and the times of the men I love: proud black gay men at war with a society that does not love them and a self they grapple to understand.

> *Black men loving Black men is the*
> *revolutionary act of the eighties . . .*
> *because as Black men we were never meant to*
> *be together—not as father and son, brother*
> *and brother—and certainly not as lovers.*[1]

144

Having survived the first decade of the AIDS pandemic and another decade of the continued assault against African peoples with my health and psyche reasonably intact, I feel fortunate. However, the uncertainty of the 1990s portends a recapitulation of past mistakes. America's soul is still ruled by the greenback, instead of higher order of thinking and a compassionate heart. And while I fight continually to escape the grasp of nihilism, it is hard to have hope in a country that has no hope for its own huddled masses yearning to be free.

> The liberal/conservative discussion conceals the most basic issues now facing black America: the nihilist threat to its very existence. This threat is not simply a matter of relative economic deprivation and political powerlessness. . . . It is primarily a question of speaking to the profound sense of psychological depression, personal worthlessness, and social despair so widespread in black America.[2]

All black Americans bring the flavor of their life trials and their history to this sense of nihilism. It does not matter if your cage is corporate America, Christopher Street, Yale, Compton, or Riker's Island. The fact still remains that we don't have 100 percent control over our lives, over our destinies, and over our individual and collective futures. Until I am privy and have access to the same resources, respect, and privileges afforded the most wealthy heterosexual white male, I'm still one of the enslaved waiting to be bought or sold.

And unfortunately, the America of the 1990s is populated by the worst sort of slaves. These aren't the field hands or even the house niggers—they all knew they were slaves. The African slaves of today deny their second-class status with Gucci labels, Ivy League educations, middle-class existences, intellectual rhetoric, and a whole host of addictions. In an America where my brothers can be killed by those who are supposed to protect them, how can I be free? In an America where my brothers and sisters have to struggle for minimal health care, even when their bodies are compromised, it's impossible not to worry and it's *damned* hard to have hope.

However,

in order for revolution to be possible, and the revolution *is* possible, it must be led by the poor and working class people of this country. Our interest does not lie with being a part of this system, and our tendencies to be co-opted and diverted are lessened by the realization of our oppression. . . . (my emphasis)[3]

At best, I've learned to keep my marching boots shined, to love my man fiercely, to lock arms with my brothers forming safe houses, and to preserve my sanity by keeping my pencil sharpened. I go on in America waiting for a revolution in consciousness, at the very least among my own.

And when I die, I do not want to be remembered by a cold headstone, a picturesque urn, or a *New York Post* headline. I want to be remembered by those things that served as my buffers against a society that taught me to deny portions of myself, a society that taught me to deny my humanity by teaching me that loving was wrong. Namely, I want to be remembered by those I have loved and the words I have left behind as testimonies—signs of my existence.

Let these very words—these very words—be the true epitaph to a life lived. They will be the final sacraments—of my life, my flesh, my blood, and my soul—that I leave to those I have loved and to posterity.

I am a black gay man. I am one of many. I have survived shit loads and I will survive even more before I finally die. I struggle daily not to be broken. I am a black gay man learning to survive in America, and these are some of my words.

NOTES

1. Joseph Beam, "Brother to Brother: Words from the Heart," *In the Life*, ed. Joseph Beam (Los Angeles: Alyson Publications, 1986), p. 240.

2. Cornel West, "The Loss of Hope," *Dissent*, Spring 1991.

3. Pat Parker, "Revolution: It's Not Neat or Pretty or Quick," *This Bridge Called My Back*, ed. Cherríe Moraga and Gloria Anzaldúa (New York: Kitchen Table, 1981), p. 240.

A PLACE AT THE ALTAR

by Lynwoodt Jenkins

"We make them doubt that they are the children of God,
and this must be the ultimate blasphemy."

—ARCHBISHOP DESMOND M. TUTU[1]

"I'm mad at God!" whispered Darryl, my best friend, who is black, gay *and* Christian. Darryl's anger erupted one afternoon upon leaving church after having sat quietly deteriorating in the pew as the minister sermonized his disgust for the (alleged) evilness of homosexuality. Darryl's words, profound and shockingly simple, reverberated to rattle in his throat, and my ears. Jumping to his feet, as if to balance his fury and brave whatever backlash that divine power would inflict, he challenged consequence. He was desperate. He had followed The Word, according to instruction. He made no errors. Calculated, by faith, no possibilities of failure. Then consoled himself into believing that abstinence, fasting, and tithing would prove a self-inflicted homo-exorcism. But it didn't work. There was no healing. There was no laying of hands. No miracles were received. Or examples to follow. Nor had there been an angelic visit expressing the significance of his fate. Most of all, there was no peace. Bereft of hope, he sobbed. The encumbering cognition of his fate left him wounded, exhausted, inextricably damaged. He had been baptized in his own tears. He was a fray in the fabric of a racist and homophobic society.

Once home, Darryl argued that he didn't request or choose his sexuality. He couldn't understand why God had allowed him to be cursed. Empathetic, I was familiar with his particular anguish all too well. He was a kindred spirit who struggled with his sexuality, as opposed to his spirituality. But there was nothing that I could've done. What he required I could not provide. It would've been arrogant to assume that an embrace would protect him. It would've been malicious to suggest that it was all an accident of nature as well as condescending to offer sympathetic words of condolence. The depth of his suffering deserved better accolades for his endurance. He had reached a crossroads of sorts, a reckoning and coming to terms with himself. That crucial and definitive hour in which one either stands valiant in fight or lays waste refusing to take arms. There is no middle ground. Sublime, it is the ultimate accountability in which we, as black gay men, must claim *a place at the altar.*

The crux of the matter is that we are the invisible soldiers. Drafted souls caught in the cross fire of a select human condition. A tumultuous battle for the merit of our lives, against the dogmatic practice and preaching of those who have damned us, adversaries who would render us silent, forsaken, and purposefully displaced.

The proverbial "black sheep" of the congregational flock. Demon savants. Tolerated *only* when measured by our octave range, athletic prowess, and/or our general public-pleasing abilities. Men who, in the light of day, are looked upon in disdain, while in the cloaking darkness of night are desired, hunted, and insulted by dead presidents in exchange for illicit favors. According to circumstantial evidence, we are the world's delicious nightmare. *This* is our dilemma.

However, we must resolve otherwise. There are no black knights in shining armor preparing for our rescues. Science cannot, and will not, produce a heterosexual antidote for us to swallow. Neither will we rise from prayer miraculously changed. Inevitably, what we must do is accept ourselves, absolute. Deliberately and reverently embracing our individual and collective exclusivity. Fully persuaded that our souls are not to be surrendered. Nor bargained. Proving greater than festering silence. More powerful than caging fear. Renewed as indestructible paragons. Warriors of the new millennium. *This* is our lot. Our duty. And, without regret, our beauty.

Therefore, for those who remain steadfast against us, perhaps a full examination of what the Bible teaches is in order. According to text, it supports the tolerance of slavery. It also supports the second-class citizenship of women. These are references that are overlooked. Or they are made malleable to accommodate a progressive society. Seemingly absurd, but accurate in context, for those who think that homosexuality is a sin and that no sin is greater or lesser than the other. With gluttony reigning as one of the seven deadliest sins, why are there no blasting and derogatory sermons for the obese? What purgatory awaits the portly members of the tabernacle? Is there no fire and brimstone for them? These factors, multiplied by the dichotomy of clandestine gay clergy members, need to be considered prior to unequivocally dismissing the children of God.

Instead, understand that whether we are black, white, gay, straight, male, female, or otherwise, we are divinely created. Our only task is to find the God within us.

Finally, my brothers, having done this purgative and needful thing, weep no more. Wipe clean the evidence of tears. Surely, given the complexity of life, that "crucial and definitive hour" is but a rite of passage toward manhood. So take heed. Load your mindful weapons, guard your newfound posts, then plant your feet on salvaged ground, and fight!

NOTE

1. From the foreword by Archbishop Desmond M. Tutu in Marilyn Bennett Alexander and James Preston, *We Were Baptized Too: Claiming God's Grace For Lesbians and Gays* (Louisville, Ky.: Westminster John Knox Press, 1996).

I Am a Homosexual

by Essex Hemphill

I am a homosexual. I love myself as a black man and homosexual. I have known since I was five that I would love men, but I did not know then that "brother," "lover," "friend" would take on more intimate and dangerous meanings. I did not know a dual oppression, a dual mockery would be practiced against me.

At nineteen, I told my parents. It was difficult for me to tell them and difficult for them to accept the news. My mother sought to blame herself, but I insisted my homosexuality is natural. My father surprised me by telling me of the pride he feels in my courage to live the life I have chosen. His support and their love and respect encourage me to aggressively pursue my human rights. My dignity.

I have not chosen to isolate myself from my friends and community. There are valid reasons for doing so, but I feel that would contribute to the absence of visible, positive homosexual images—particularly images for the young, who must still discover their sexual identities awkwardly, dangerously, or sadly.

Unlike some of my brothers who shun the responsibility of relationships with women or seek only the company of men, I have not found either extreme to be fulfilling. It has proven to be rewarding for me to stay in touch with women, to nurture friendships with them as close as family ties. I have learned that sensitivity is natural, not sissy. I have yet to understand why emotional expression by men must be understated or under control when the process of living requires the capacity to feel and express. Sharing with women has helped me form an androgynous sensibility through which I create and perceive my experiences. It allows me to respect individual differences, powers, and points of view and to forge alliances that extremes of sexual exclusion would not allow. But learning to conduct worthwhile relationships with women has not been painless. I have learned from losing dear friends how to better the quality of my next relationships and those that now exist.

I have not found loving a man easy either, but I do not fool myself and consider that loving a woman would be easier. Once I move beyond sexual impulse, there has to exist a compatibility of spirit. Just because I am attracted to some members of my own sex does not mean I will know how to love. Learning to compromise, learning to support one another, learning to share power instead of ruling one another by it are the challenges I have found in my relationships with men. In loving a black man I feel I love a comrade. I look for strength in my lovers and define it succinctly as being able to deal in the truth. Candor has become a necessary part of loving not just a man, but any and all whom I love.

My women friends who are not homosexual have remarked about how many of us homosexual men there appear to be. One girlfriend feels all the best men she could court and marry are homosexual. She bases her comments on observing homosexual men as being sensitive, well-groomed, and articulate. I have warned her of the danger she places herself in by believing such a generalization—she will frustrate her ability to relate intimately with heterosexual men if she believes that she is accepting less than what she wants. I would be irresponsible to encourage her to continue believing homosexual men are in any way superior to heterosexual men. I believe the ideal "We are equal," even though this ideal is not always practiced in my favor.

Some men and women will consider me a "lost brother," "the enemy," or a "brainwashed victim." To them I respond: I have as much strength as you. In my heart. In my mind. In my hands. I am equal to father, brother, stranger. I am not the enemy. I am a black man who is nurtured intimately by loving other men. But I am not so completely fulfilled that I must shut out the rest of the world.

In choosing not to isolate myself, I am isolated. Ironically, this is the foremost risk in choosing to live openly, but it is also a reason I am disappointed in and disillusioned with the gay community and the gay rights movement. The gay community is divided by racist and sexist practices and attitudes that are perpetuated by members of the community. The gay rights movement has been generally unreceptive to black involvement in its political activities and insensitive to black concerns. The gay rights movement has also been depicted by the media, both general and gay, as a white male, middle-class movement. The gay ghettoes, such as Castro Street in San Francisco, are like small compact mirrors that do not reflect a total view of the homosexual experience and its relationship to the world. The term "gay," as it is commonly used by the media and the movement, generally excludes black homosexuals. The term also excludes *all* homosexual women, who are secondly identified as "lesbian." These contradictions cause me to view the gay rights movement as an insincere human rights struggle.

I believe the task for the politically active, courageous black homosexual who has not chosen to be isolated is to begin to sensitize our families, friends, and communities to our concerns and to create images of ourselves in true proportion to who we are. The community in general is widely misinformed about us to the degree that mythology *is* accepted as fact. The black community cannot afford to indulge in excluding black homosexuals or in condemning us. Nor can black homosexuals afford the exclusive, powerless indulgence of being a subculture, fearful and unwilling to defend our right to legitimate human rights and dignity.

· V ·
LEGACY

BECOMING A MOVEMENT

by Rodney Christopher

The sociopolitical movement of African-American gay men is largely a result of historical change in American society regarding the questions of race, gender, and sexual orientation. Unlike white gays and lesbians who began organizing politically in the United States in the 1950s, black gay men and lesbians could not consider their sexual orientation to be a part of their personal and political identity, and, more important, they could not recognize the importance of organizing on both their race and sexual orientation, until African Americans had gained the legislative rights and economic opportunities won because of the civil rights movement of the 1950s and 1960s. After that time, it was the effort and oversights of the gay rights movement and the women's movement that demonstrated the importance of organizing African-American lesbians and gay men.

Racism is extremely pervasive. Although slavery ended officially in 1863, for the next century Jim Crow laws and practices legitimized the separation of public accommodations and communities along racial lines in the South. The North was not extremely different. There African Americans were not allowed to live in many places because of racism, instead forming what are now called inner cities or rural pockets. The result of such rigid segregation can be seen by looking at the current economic position and health status of African Americans.

Because race has been such a huge determining factor of one's life chances, colored or Negro or black has been, for most

African Americans, the most important factor in the shaping of our identity as human beings. The overwhelming historical significance of race, then, has made it virtually impossible for the large part of the community of black gay men and lesbians to consider their sexuality as integral to their identity, especially on a political—that is, public—level. They have had to see their sexual orientation as private and secondary.

Being homosexual, regardless of race, is a taboo in a great many parts of the world. (The terms *gay* and *lesbian* themselves are political and were not used frequently before the late 1960s. Prior to this, the common term was *homosexual*.) There have been, and still are, very strict antisodomy laws on the books in many states and countries, and the antihomosexual influence in the Bible, with the story of Sodom and Gomorrah and several lines in the book of Leviticus, has greatly affected the codes of living in Western society.

Nonetheless, homosexuals have not always conformed to those societal rules that have attempted to deny their existence and persecute them. Many have made great strides toward changing them, mostly within Western, or capitalist, society. Historian Barry D. Adam, in *The Rise of a Gay and Lesbian Movement*, argues that capitalist society created the preconditions that led to the lesbian and gay sociopolitical movement in the United States and parts of Europe. He suggests that the tendency of capitalist society to create massive social mobility and to allow for the possibility of living away from large families created a homosexual subculture and its subsequent sociopolitical movement.

For many years, as far back as the 1700s in Europe, there has been a primarily white homosexual subculture in Western cities. It is marked by bars and social clubs mostly for men. Women sometimes frequented these bars, but were generally the minority. Those who discovered their homosexuality knew that they would not be accepted into the mainstream of society, and instead they began to create spaces in which they could be relatively comfortable with their sexuality. Their comfort was limited because the bars were frequently raided by the police, and people were often arrested for patronizing them.

It was this limited comfort that later led some lesbians and gay men to form organizations to gain rights for themselves.

African-American homosexuals—both men and women—were indeed a part of this phenomenon; several bars that arose in the United States had a largely black homosexual clientele. One city that became notorious for its black nightlife and culture was New York City. By the end of the nineteenth century, Harlem was the cultural base of the African-American community. The longest continuously operating gay events in American history were the lavish black homosexual drag balls in Harlem that began in the 1890s. The Savoy Ballroom, originally at Lenox Avenue and 140th Street, was known to house these gala events in the 1920s.

There are both positive and negative consequences to the emergence of this homosexual subculture. The creation of private spaces like bars gave people opportunity to spend their leisure time comfortably as openly lesbian or gay. In these social settings people can let go of the facade of being "straight"; within their subculture, people are free to be themselves. However, while it is clear that the homosexual subculture had to be hidden, the mere existence of a subculture maintains the premise that being gay or lesbian is at best a "private" issue, and at worst a cause for self-hatred.

Despite the safety of being hidden, both from the larger society and the black community, there have been times in the history of African Americans when individual people who were gay or lesbian (or bisexual) have become public figures. However, these individuals have been recognized for their contributions to the black community: The black community has generally avoided the question of their sexuality and the individuals themselves have chosen not to be politically gay.

The Harlem Renaissance was one such period. From roughly 1919 to 1934, Harlem presented an opportunity for members of the growing Negro elite to express themselves. Several members of this elite were gay or lesbian, and, while their sexuality was certainly not sanctioned, it was tolerated by their contemporaries: "Rumors aside, Harlem always ignored or forgave everything of its best and brightest," wrote the historian David Levering Lewis in his book *When Harlem Was in Vogue.*[1]

Many of the artists and writers who became famous during the Harlem Renaissance did so with the help of an influential group of philanthropists known as "The Six": Jessie Redmon Fauset, Charles Johnson, Alain Locke, Walter White, Casper Holstein, and James Weldon Johnson. Each of these people had the means to give "emergency loans and temporary beds, professional advice and Downtown contracts, prizes and publicity,"[2] to struggling talents. They were all members of the Harlem elite, each having a prestigious college education, and they were relatively wealthy—some more than others. "Without these six, the Harlem roster of 26 novels, ten volumes of poetry, five Broadway plays, innumerable essays and short stories, two or three performed ballets and concerti, and the large output of canvas and sculpture would have been a great deal shorter."[3]

Alain Locke, who was more capable of offering financial assistance to Harlem Renaissance artists than all but one of "The Six," was a black gay man. Locke's father was a member of the fourth class to graduate from Howard University's law department. Locke was a magna cum laude graduate of Harvard University, the first African-American Rhodes scholar at Oxford University, and, later, a professor at Howard. He was also a good friend of W.E.B. DuBois; Locke and DuBois "were among the most scrupulously educated Americans."[4]

In 1925, Locke's *The New Negro*, an anthology of work by thirty-four African Americans and four whites, was published. The theme of the anthology was based on Locke's "conviction that the race's 'more immediate hope rests in the revelation by white and black alike of the Negro in terms of his artistic endowments and cultural contributions, past and prospective.' "[5] As a result of the book, the term the New Negro began to be used to describe the cultural elite who, like Locke, seemed to believe that racism could be ended by generating universal respect for the cultural expressions of blacks. Locke's contribution, like that of most everyone involved in the Harlem Renaissance, was to the black community at large. While those who knew him well were aware that he was a homosexual,

Locke's gayness was never a part of his political and public identity.

Perhaps the most noted of those whom Locke assisted was James Mercer Langston Hughes. Hughes is one of the most revered black writers of all time. His poems are included in all kinds of anthologies, both "American" and African American. One of his most famous pieces is a short poem called "I, too." Its theme is a call for the world to recognize that African Americans are not invisible, that they are part of the United States. The first line reads "I, too sing America," the last states "I, too am American." Because Hughes never married and was very good friends with several men known to be homosexual, speculation about his sexuality has been widespread. While no one is certain, several historians claim that it is very likely that he, too, sang black gay American.

The first piece of fiction to explore the theme of black homosexuality was published during the Harlem Renaissance; its writer was Richard Bruce Nugent. In 1926, his short story "Smoke, Lilies, and Jade" was published in the short-lived journal *Fire!!* This short story was reprinted in *Black Men/White Men: A Gay Anthology* and is mentioned in both Joseph Beam's *In the Life: A Black Gay Anthology* and *Other Countries: Black Gay Voices*, the latter two being significant contributions to a recent surge in published black gay male literature. There were several other talents from the Harlem Renaissance who were African-American homosexual men and women, but that is outside the scope of this essay.

The next period that held significance for the growing group consciousness of black gay men and lesbians was the civil rights movement. It was during these years that the emergence of James Baldwin created some turmoil in the social fabric of American culture. Baldwin's *Giovanni's Room*, published in 1956 and set in Paris, is a story of love between men. Perhaps the most controversial piece of writing on the issue of race that has been published in the United States was his *The Fire Next Time*, published in 1963. It was in this work that Baldwin called upon his nephew to ". . . accept them [whites] . . . accept them with love. For these innocent people have no other hope. They are, in effect still trapped in a history which they do not understand."

Unfortunately for the community of African-American gay men and lesbians, Baldwin was not politically gay; in an interview with the editor of *The Black Scholar*, he stated: "I love men but I am not homosexual." He insisted that his sexuality was a private matter, either unwilling or unable to recognize the significance of being "out." While he did realize that people who were black and gay, a word whose meaning he "never really understood" were at a greater disadvantage than white gays, he never took on that reality as a political issue worthy of his energies.

But this is not to underestimate the significance of James Baldwin for the community of black gay men and lesbians. Despite his insistence that his gayness should remain private, Baldwin was never afraid to say that he loved men; neither was he afraid to write about it. In 1979, Baldwin completed and published the first full-length novel that deals with the experience of black gay men in the United States, *Just Above My Head*. Bayard Rustin was also a major figure during the civil rights movement. He was the principal organizer for the 1963 March on Washington. Most of the country was not privy to the knowledge of Rustin's sexual orientation, but many of the leaders of the civil rights movement did know of it. Unfortunately, but not surprisingly, the leaders asked Rustin to keep his "private" life private; the "black" agenda had to be pushed first. Fortunately, in 1985, Rustin began to speak out about being black and gay. Before his death in 1987, he had done full-length interviews for at least two important publications in the black lesbian and gay community, *Black/Out* and *Other Countries: Black Gay Voices*.

At approximately the same time that the civil rights movement was forging ahead to end racism, a movement for homosexual rights was working to end homophobia in the United States. The "homophile" movement, as it was called, was made up of organizations in several cities, the most well known of which were the Mattachine Society, a national organization comprised primarily of white gay men that began in Los Angeles in 1951 and had chapters in several major cities, and the Daughters of Bilitis (DOB), a similar organization comprised primarily of white lesbians that began in San Francisco in 1955. The most significant contribution of this movement was that it gave people an opportunity to begin to question the idea that homosexuality is taboo.

The homophile movement, while it made some strides, was largely a conservative and assimilationist, middle-to-upper class, white male movement. The Mattachine Society spent much of its energy trying to convince homosexuals that the road to equality was to "stress the common humanity of homosexuals and heterosexuals and keep sexuality as such private," while DOB included in its objectives "advocating a mode of behavior and dress acceptable to society," "participation in research projects," and "investigation of the penal code as it pertains to the homosexual . . . and promotion of these changes through the due process of law in the state legislatures." The leaders of the homophile movement were unwilling to accept homosexuals who frequented "the bar scene" and generally treated them as second-class homosexuals. This did not help to generate a mass movement because most of the people who would have been likely to join the movement were those who went to the bars.

The time began to change when, on a hot June night in New York City in 1969, one of the less "classy" gay bars that was frequented by African-American and Latino lesbians and gays was the target of a police raid, a long-standing tradition of New York's Finest. "The Stonewall Riots" lasted for two nights and, because of their militancy, they are seen as the impetus for the modern gay rights, gay pride movement. The sheer strength displayed at Stonewall helped to give gays and lesbians the inspiration to begin addressing a more radical agenda than the homophile movement did.

Despite the contribution that African Americans and Latinos made to starting the gay rights movement, that movement did not make much of an effort to respond to the problems and needs of gays and lesbians of color. Like its predecessor the homophile movement, this new movement was quickly dominated by white gay men. As the gay pride movement progressed, black lesbians and gays and white lesbians began to realize that while the leadership may have shared their com-

mon interest in ending homophobia, these white male leaders
were not as interested in giving up the power that their whiteness and maleness afforded them in American society.

As a result, several splits in political organization began to
happen in the early 1970s. Sexism in the gay pride movement
and homophobia in the women's movement led to a lesbian and
radical lesbian movement. As a result of an increase in blacks
earning a college education in the 1970s—which was in large
part due to Affirmative Action, a product of the civil rights movement—a growing number of African Americans became involved
in lesbian and gay politics. In the face of racism in the gay pride
movement, the women's movement, and the lesbian movement,
both black gay men and lesbians—separately and in coalition—
found the need to organize separately from whites and men.

Along with racism, black lesbians also faced the sexism of
black gay men and the homophobia of some black feminists,
and they realized that they experienced all the major oppres-
sions (racism, classism, sexism, and homophobia) that led to a
further split in the development of the black lesbian female and
black gay male communities. In fact, the oldest organization for
African-American homosexuals is African-American Wimmin
United for Societal Change, which began as Salsa Soul Sisters
in 1975. Today the organization is called African Ancestral Lesbians United for Societal Change (AALUSC).

Most of the growth, therefore, that has taken place in the
community of black gay men and lesbians in the United States
is a very recent, and organizationally complex, development.
Nineteen seventy-eight marked the beginning of a new era of
trust. It was during this year that black gays and lesbians
joined forces separate from the larger lesbian and gay and
black movements to form what was then called the National
Coalition of Black Gays. (In 1985, the name was changed to
the National Coalition of Black *Lesbians and* Gays [NCBLG].)
NCBG took advantage of the October 1979 March on Washington for Lesbian and Gay Rights to hold the first National Third
World Lesbian and Gay Conference. In 1980, black gay men
joined forces with white gay men to create the National Association of Black and White Men Together/Men of All Colors
Together. Chapters of this organization currently exist in over

twenty U.S. cities and at least two foreign countries. Several organizations solely for African-American gay men have come and gone, with at least Gay Men of African Descent in New York City (1986), Adodi in Philadelphia (1986), and the Black Men's Xchange in California (1989) remaining.

The threat that AIDS has imposed upon all gay men and the entire African-American community has been, perhaps, the most important contributing factor to the recent growth in the sociopolitical movement of African-American gay men. Watching their friends die and knowing that several of them would die soon, combined with the nationwide hysteria that aroused more homophobic discrimination and violence, led many gay men and lesbians of all races to become politically involved. Sociopolitical organizations provided a forum for support and an opportunity to plan ways to get funding for AIDS research and services and medication for those who could not afford them.

The 1980s has seen a strong effort on the parts of African-American gay men, both individually and collectively, to "come out of the closet" in a society where, as the writer Joseph Beam—a hero and pioneer of the community of black gay men—puts it, "Visibility is survival." It was during the mid-to-late 1980s that black gay men developed a level of group consciousness that led them to form organizations solely for themselves, to work more with black lesbians and with white gay men, and to express in writing, photography, theatre, and film the experience of the community of African-American gay men in the United States.

NOTES

1. David Levering Lewis, *When Harlem Was in Vogue* (New York: Vintage Books, paperback, 1982), p. 76.

2. Ibid., p. 120.

3. Ibid., p. 121.

4. Ibid., p. 150.

5. Ibid., p. 117.

THE TRUTH ABOUT STONEWALL

by Mark Haile

June 27, 1969, the Stonewall Inn at 53 Christopher Street, in Greenwich Village, New York City.

It was described as "the hairpin drop heard around the world," in reference to a 1960s expression for revealing you were gay before "coming out of the closet" was fashionable. Until Stonewall, gay people were either "out" only to one another or they were yanked out of the closet by scandal, destined for shame, humiliation, and ruin.

But Stonewall changed all of that. Something happened in New York's West Village at what had been a shabby little bar off Sheridan Square that would influence nearly every lesbian and gay man living in America today.

The impact of what happened at the Stonewall Inn has been overrated, some critics say. Yet veterans of the gay pride movement note with amusement how many people claim to have been there and to have been part of the riots of June 27, 28, and 29.

In the retelling of the tale, history has become myth and desperation is remembered as romance. Changes and omissions, whether accidental or intentional, are nothing new in American history when it concerns people of color, gays, or women.

And the Stonewall legend does concern people of color. If that sultry weekend's street theatre is to be regarded as the launching pad of the modern gay rights movement, then it is essential for us to know the key players who started it all: drag queens, hustlers, jailbait juveniles, and gay men and lesbians of color. The outcasts of gay life thus showed homosexual America how to make a fist, fight back, and win self-respect.

The Stonewall was certainly not the first bar of its kind to cater to the "fringe element" of the gay community. Interracial bars and bars geared toward blacks and Latinos in New York City had been around for well over fifty years.

In the decade prior to the Depression, Harlem enjoyed the title of Negro capital of the United States—home to the nation's most talented black artists, writers, and musicians. Clubs like the Hot Cha and Lulu Belle's rivaled the best bars of today's gay scene. The Savoy Ballroom, originally at Lenox Avenue and 140th Street, was the hot spot in the 1920s for the black gay drag balls that had been in existence since the 1890s, making them the longest continously operating gay event in American history.

By that muggy summer of 1969, however, Harlem was scarcely the mecca for America's black cultural elite.

It was hot and humid day and night that Friday, June 27, as it had been and would be for weeks on end.

Gay bars had a short life span in the sixties. Election year would precipitate raids on a regular basis. Developers used heavy-handed methods to get hold of desirable property. The mob looked on popular gay bars as targets for takeover. Rarely was there any resistance to any of these threats—especially when bar owners also had to pay out to the cop on the beat just to stay in existence.

Bars with a black lesbian and gay following opened and closed on a regular basis all over New York City. In the Village, they were usually racially mixed bars like the Grapevine or Gianni's; the clubs in Harlem were usually all black, but they tended to blend straight and gay clientele, like Snookie's, the Purple Manor, and the Dug Out, to name a few.

Jack, a dapper, white-haired gentleman, fondly remembers bars where "everyone wore a tie. You had to be so careful in those days. If you were a stranger in the bar, no one would speak to you until they checked you out. Then once they knew you were okay, they were the friendliest people you could ever meet."

Larry Boxx, who ran the Stonewall at the time of the riots, worked in or owned more than a dozen bars in his day in the club business in New York. He remembers the era before the riots at the Stonewall vividly.

"I was arrested 109 times, with only three convictions. It was a game. Police would check up on business licenses constantly. There was a [Deputy Inspector] Pine who really had it in for the gay clubs," he recalls. Pine was a deputy inspector from the public morals section of the New York Police Department. A typical violation would be for something like no soap in the men's room or an unlicensed coat checkroom.

"I once had eight raids in one night. I had a charge account with bail bondsmen," Boxx recalls. Standard procedure was to take down to the precinct the manager on duty or a staff member, who would usually be processed and back to work in a few minutes. "You took a token bust," Boxx recalls.

A black Los Angeles psychologist remembers an experience in a gay club before the Stonewall riots. "You couldn't even touch another man in those days! A drag queen tried to give me a kiss once, and the undercover cop went "Whoosh!" and snatched her up and hauled her off to jail. I didn't have any ID on me. I was underage and when the police weren't looking, the other queens hissed at me, 'Run, run like your life depends on it.' And I did, too. We couldn't dance together, you know. There was a big light on top of the jukebox. When the police would come through the door, this bright light would come on, and everybody would grab the nearest girl to dance with, that's just the way it was."

At one point in 1969, there was only one dance bar for gays in Manhattan. "Six months in the bar business was a long time," Larry Boxx recounts.

The Stonewall Inn scarcely reflected the refinement of the gay bars that had been evident during the Harlem Renaissance. As dance bars today go, it was fairly simple.

In the 1950s, according to Boxx, the Stonewall Inn had been an elegant dinner house, with an enormous flagstone fireplace.

A long bar dominated the far right wall of the two adjoining storefronts that made up the interior.

The Stonewall Inn had gone through a succession of owners through the late fifties and sixties as the area around Sheridan Square fell upon hard times.

The bar eventually garnered a gay clientele, but not of the sport coat and tie set. Even as the riots were getting under way in defense of the Stonewall, there was another effort under way elsewhere to start a boycott against it and other bars like it. Shabby gay bars like the Stonewall were perceived by some as more of a threat to the health and self-image of lesbians and gays than the safe haven from persecution they offered.

The late Craig Rodwell, founder of the Oscar Wilde Memorial Bookshop in the Village, recalled that between the police and the Mafia, no one could open a gay bar in 1968 with "a healthy social atmosphere." The Stonewall was suspected of being responsible for a local outbreak of hepatitis because bar backs didn't bother washing the glasses.

The crowd that weekend was anything but politically charged. But it was hot. More than twenty thousand people had waited up to four hours to view the body of Judy Garland, an icon among many gay men, at the Frank Campbell Funeral Home at Eighty-first Street and Madison Avenue. Thousands of black people came to pay their respects, too—young and old, men and women. Many people took Friday off to go see her. Thousands filled the streets afterward, with time on their hands and nothing to do. The journalist Charles Kaiser states in his book *The Gay Metropolis: 1940–1996*, that "No one will ever know for sure which was the most important reason for what happened next: the freshness in their minds of Judy Garland's funeral, or the example of all the previous rebellions of the sixties—the civil rights revolution, the sexual revolution and the psychedelic revolution, each of which had punctured gaping holes in crumbling traditions of passivity, puritanism and bigotry."[1]

When Deputy Inspector Pine and the seven other policemen from the public morals section set out that night for the

Stonewall, it was to have been a routine raid like the several others that had preceded it in the weeks before.

Boxx recalls that the only thing actually amiss at the Stonewall Inn was a $20 tax stamp that the bar was supposed to have on record. The search warrant brought by Pine was for investigation of reports that liquor was being sold illegally, that the club was operating without a license.

Sometime after Friday night became early Saturday morning, the police began their raid of the bar that they referred to as "well known for its homosexual clientele." Upon serving the warrant, detectives began taking inventory of the liquor they were about to confiscate. Patrons were usually allowed to leave after their ID was checked, except those "suspected of cross-dressing," who were to be taken to the precinct house for questioning and eventually released.

Those permitted out of the bar by the police milled about outside, standing by Sheridan Square, waiting for friends still inside the bar.

There had been about two hundred people inside the Stonewall, but now the crowd had doubled in size as passersby watched the show, and those exiting the bar shouted and shrieked to their friends, posing grandly.

Some bar patrons were apprehensive because of events surrounding raids days earlier. Among those who had been arrested was a young South American student, fearful of being deported if it was discovered he was gay. Despondent, he leapt from the third-story window of the Charles Street stationhouse while in custody, impaling himself on the spikes atop the facility's surrounding wrought-iron fence. Although he survived the fall, he was maimed for life, and sensational photographs of the incident made the front pages of the New York tabloids. For the homosexual community, it inflamed an already long, hot summer. It was prominent in the conversations of those waiting for their friends still inside the bar.

The mood shifted quickly when three drag queens were taken from the bar and placed in a police van. The crowd began shouting at the policemen, but the real confrontation was yet to take place.

The next person taken out of the bar was a lesbian, who

struggled with the police every step of the way. This seemed to be the visual cue that motivated the crowd, for no one person led the charge. No one directed the energy of the throng.

What happened next was described as "a rampage" by *The New York Times*. The crowd started throwing everything and anything they could get their hands on at the startled police.

Larry Boxx remembers that there was a loose parking meter that was uprooted easily as the policemen barricaded themselves inside the bar amid a shower of pennies, bricks, and bottles.

Tactical Patrol Force (TPF) units, a new antiriot squad designed specifically for use in Harlem, were brought in to clear the area. Eventually thirteen people were arrested that evening with four policemen reported slightly injured.

When the Stonewall reopened the following night serving only soft drinks, the TPF units appeared shortly after two A.M. to clear the crowd that had gathered along Christopher Street and in Sheridan Square.

The riot squad, linked arm to arm the width of the street, dispersed the crowd between Sixth and Seventh Avenues. Those who didn't escape down the numerous narrow alleys and side streets in time were clubbed and shoved to the ground. This time only three people were arrested, but many more were injured or involved in the confrontation as the police broke ranks and charged into the crowd.

On the second night of fighting with the police, gay graffiti appeared all over the street and the shouts included "Gay power!" Numerous flyers were passed out among the crowd.

Even though they started out as an unruly mob without direction or leadership, something emerged and electrified those who were present. The lesbians and gay men who filled Sheridan Square became empowered by their own hands.

The Inn remained closed after the riots, covered with slogans such as "Gay Rights Now" and "Legalize Gay Bars."

In 1972, Larry Boxx had to leave New York City because of investigations by the Knapp Commission regarding corruption in the NYPD. Ironically, Boxx served as Grand Marshal

of the Long Beach (California) Gay Pride Parade in commemo-
ration of the twentieth anniversary of the Stonewall riots.

There were gay organizations already in existence at the
time of Stonewall: the cautious and conservative Mattachine
Society, with chapters nationwide, and the more radical Student Homophile League at Columbia University. Still, it took
those who had the least to lose, the black and Latino drag
queens, to forgo "acceptable behavior" and reject obedience to
authority to become catalysts for the birth of the modern gay
pride movement.

Their model was neither the hesitant nor the rash assertion
of their self-proclaimed leadership, but the fury, desperation,
and pride aborning of the militant black power movement. In
1969, many were giving up powerlessness. And they were, or
were following, African Americans.

Since the Stonewall riots, many organizations have used
the Stonewall name in tribute to the importance of the event.
Many individuals active in the lesbian and gay movement remember when they first heard about the Stonewall riots, and
a few even have authentic personal recollections of the events.
Yet no group or individual can claim responsibility for the
resistance offered that weekend. The credit belongs to a handful of people who have since been forgotten, jettisoned by a
movement that more and more reflects conformity as the
years pass.

The names of those who fought that first battle for gay
rights have largely passed into obscurity, yet their legacy has
been embraced by the entire nation's gay community, with a
profound effect on the course of the lives of millions. When
former president Ronald Reagan used the phrase that he "came
out of the closet" (as an opera lover) on nationwide television
a few years ago, he had no idea of the origin of the expression
he was using, so popular has its usage become.

As the lesbian writer Jane Rule said, lesbians and gay men
have a gift of love to give to the entire world; so, too, did
those anonymous black and Latino gay men and lesbians at

the Stonewall Inn give the precious gift of life to an entire movement.

When the movement began the rule was inclusiveness rather than separation, so unlike many of today's lesbian and gay institutions. Hopefully, the lesbian and gay community will become ever more aware of its roots, that the spirit of the first warriors of our modern movement will offer guidance and aid in the battles yet to come.

NOTE

1. Charles Kaiser, *The Gay Metropolis: 1940–1996* (Boston: Houghton Mifflin, 1997), p. 197.

CONTRIBUTORS

MARK SIMMONS, an Arkansan by birth, is a writer currently living in Los Angeles. Simmons's short stories, journalism, and poetry have appeared in *Alternatives, SBC, Emerge, Ecce Queer, Spin, Kuumba, The Advocate,* and the *James White Review.*

KHEVEN L. LAGRONE lives and writes in Oakland, California. He has an interest in African-American genealogy and history. His writings have appeared in *SBC* magazine, *Whazzup!* magazine, the *San Francisco Sentinel,* the *Bay Area Reporter,* and the anthology *River Crossings: Voices of the Diaspora* (International Black Writers and Artists, Los Angeles). "From my great-great-great-great grandfather to my nephews (eight generations) we have been 'the African,' 'Free Men of Color,' 'Mulatto,' 'Colored,' 'Negro,' then black, Afro-, and African American. These terms are part of my black male heritage. For me, the new term 'black man who loves black men' most strongly embraces this heritage."

GEOFFREY GIDDINGS was born in Georgetown, Guyana, in 1966 and moved to Brooklyn, New York, in 1980. He completed undergraduate studies in African-American Studies at Brandeis University in 1990 and is currently a graduate student at Temple University. He resides in Philadelphia.

REGINALD SHEPHERD was born in New York City in 1963 and raised in the Bronx. He received his B.A. from Bennington College in 1988 and his M.F.A. degrees from Brown University in 1991 and the University of Iowa in 1993.

His work has appeared in *Grand Street, The Iowa Review, The Kenyon Review, The Nation, The Paris Review, Poetry, Tri-Quarterly*, and many other journals. He was a contributor of *In the Life: A Black Gay Anthology* (Alyson, 1986). The University of Pittsburgh Press published his first book, *Some Are Drowning*, in 1994 as winner of the 1993 Associated Writing Programs' Award Series in Poetry. His second book, *Angel, Interrupted*, was published by the University of Pittsburgh Press in 1996; it was a finalist for a 1997 Lambda Literary Award in Gay Male Poetry. The University of Pittsburgh Press will publish his third book, *Wrong*, in the spring of 1999.

Shepherd lives in Chicago and teaches at Northern Illinois University.

EDWIN L. GREENE was born in Cincinnati, Ohio, on August 23, 1952, and has lived in that city "all my life. I founded a local group called the Black Gay Men's Support Group in my living room in October 1987. Several years later, we changed our name to Brothers for Brothers. We stopped meeting in 1992. Someone else picked it up with some of the old faces, plus some new ones and a new name: Brother to Brother. The concept of black gay male brotherhood continues to survive in Cincinnati. I consider myself, if we are to use labels, an African-American gay activist. Meaning that I want African-American gay men to love themselves and each other."

JOSEPH F. BEAM was a Philadelphia writer and editor. His essays appeared in the *Philadelphia Gay News, Au Courant, Blackheart 3: The Telling of Us*, among other publications. He was also the editor of the much acclaimed black gay anthology, *In the Life* (Alyson, 1986).

Beam died of AIDS-related complications in 1988.

THOM BEAN was born in 1944 in Nashville, Tennessee. He lived in Nashville, Chicago, New York City, and San Francisco, where he made his home for fourteen years. An activist in the gay community since the early days of gay liberation, he was a founding member and the first chairman of Black and White Men Together/San Francisco Bay Area (BWMT/SFBA). Bean also served as Third World cochair of the San Francisco Gay Pride Committee, president of San Francisco Girth and Mirth, interim cochair with Carole Migden of the Coalition for Human Rights, director of OUT/LOOK Foundation Board, and cofacilitator with Pat Norman of Racism and Homophobia in the Media. He served as a director on Gay and Lesbian Allegiance Against Defamation/SFBA, as a national representative to GLAAD/USA, and as director on the national board of NABWMT.

Bean's writing was first published by the *Windy City Times* in Chicago. After that Bean's work appeared in *The Advocate*, *AdWeek*, *OUT/LOOK*, the *New York Native*, *NYQ*, *QW*, *Outlines*, the *Bay Area Reporter*, the *San Francisco Sentinel*, the *San Francisco Chronicle*, and the *San Francisco Bay Times*, in which he wrote a popular column. He also appeared in the following anthologies: *Black Men/White Men*, NABWMT's *Resisting Racism*, *The Road Before Us*, and *Milking Black Bull: 11 Gay Black Poets* (the last two were edited by Assotto Saint). In the early 1980s, Bean published a merchant/consumer vehicle called the *Castro Express.*

Bean died of a heart attack in his home in San Francisco in 1996.

KEVIN MCGRUDER is a resident of Harlem. He is the executive director of Gay Men of African Descent (GMAD), a social services organization based in New York City. His writings have appeared in the *New York Amsterdam News*, *Sojourner: Black Gay voices in the Age of AIDS*, and *The Black Scholar.*

SUR RODNEY (SUR) is a writer and artist living in New York City as well as in London and Cape Breton Island, Canada. A native of Montreal, and an honors graduate of the Montreal Museum of Fine Arts School of Art & Design Studio program, Sur moved to New York in 1976 to pursue his interest with multimedia installations, fine art consulting, and the packaging and presentation of his ideas.

Within the black gay community, he was one of the more active members of a collective of black gay writers and multimedia performance artists known as Blackheart Collective, founded in 1980. His writing is included in the Blackheart's premiere issue *Yemanja* and years later in the Lambda Literary Award–winning Galiens Press publication *The Road Before Us*, edited by Assotto Saint. He is an active participant in Other Countries, a black gay men's writing workshop, and he will be published in *Other Countries Anthology III.* Sur is currently writing a book on the queer East Village art scene of the 1980s.

EUGENE HARRIS was born on January 27, 1959, in Chicago, Illinois. He grew up on the streets until he was confined to the St. Charles, Illinois, juvenile detention center. Since the age of nineteen he has been in several Illinois Department of Corrections facilities.

G. WINSTON JAMES is a poet and short-story writer living in Brooklyn, New York. He is the coeditor of *Kuumba*, the African-American lesbian and gay poetry journal. James is also the executive director of Other Countries: Black Gay Expression, a writing collective. His poetry has appeared in *The Road Before Us: 100 Gay Black Poets* and *Sojourner: Black Gay Voices in the Age of AIDS.* His short story "Church" was published in *Shade: An Anthology of Fiction by Gay Men of African Descent* (Avon Books).

R. LEIGH (TRÉ) JOHNSON was a native of Atlanta, Georgia, where he resided. He was a performing artist in poetry and song. He was the author of the play "The Life . . . Legends Past and Present." Johnson was one of the authors of a collection of works entitled *Souls on Fire.* The founder of Sissy Shocker's, a theatre troupe of gay and bisexual African-American men, he was a noted activist in Atlanta. Johnson died of AIDS-related complications in 1996.

TOD A. ROULETTE is a writer living in New York City. He is a native of Kansas, where he earned his B.A. in American Studies and art history from the University of Kansas.

His articles have appeared in *Fad*, *QW*, *The Paper*, and *Poz*, among other publications.

DONALD KEITH JACKSON, born in North Carolina, served honorably in the United States Marine Corps. He currently lives in New York City, where he is pursuing his B.A./M.A. in liberal studies at the New School for Social Research. He is an avid reader of James Baldwin's books and a longtime connoisseur of Johnny Mathis's music.

JALAL was awarded three consecutive merit scholarships (from 1984 to 1986) to the Cranbrook Writers Conference at the world-renowned Cranbrook Academy in Michigan. While there, he studied under Diane Wakoski, David Ignatow, and Judith Mintz.

Jalal helped to establish Men of Color Detroit and founded the Black Gay Brotherhood of Cleveland. He most recently had work anthologized in *Apocalypse*. Jalal has publicly read his work in Detroit, Cleveland, and Washington, D.C., where he currently resides.

RODNEY MCCOY, JR. is an African-American/Native American writer and health educator. A native New Yorker, McCoy received his B.A. from Oberlin College. Writing since age eleven, McCoy has been published in *The Road Before Us*, *Sojourner: Black Gay Voices in the Age of AIDS*, *Buti Voxx*, and *JFY* magazine. He also volunteers for People of Color in Crisis, Inc., doing HIV education and training. McCoy lives in Brooklyn, New York, and is the founder of RJM Productions, a theatrical production company. He is also working on a novel and an anthology of black gay erotica.

ROBERT E. PENN has published poetry and prose in *Essence* magazine, *The Portable Lower East Side*, *new africa*, *queer city issues*, and other journals. His work is featured in the anthologies, *The Road Before Us: 100 Gay Black Poets* and *Sojourner: Black Gay Voices in the Age of AIDS*. He is also the author of *The Gay Men's Wellness Guide* (Owl Books/Henry Holt, 1998).

ARNOLD JACKSON was diagnosed HIV-positive in June 1991. He was a longtime activist in the African-American gay community and participated in such past organizations as Philadelphia Black Gays and Innerpride. He was also a frequent contributor to and former editor of *Colours* magazine, a publication for progressive men of color.

Jackson, who held a B.A. from Temple University's School of Communications and Theatre, also portrayed "Bert" in the local production of "Jerker," a critically acclaimed two-man play on the early years of the AIDS epidemic, produced by Philadelphia's Avalanche Theatre Company in June 1992.

He was the recipient of the 1993 *Philadelphia Gay News* Lambda Award for "Distinguished Service by an Individual— Male" and a 1993 Community Service Award from Men of All Colors Together (MACT) for "providing a positive gay image and AIDS/HIV education to the general public."

Jackson was a longtime proponent of holistic approaches to AIDS and other health concerns.

He was a resident of Philadelphia, the City of Brotherly Love. He died there in 1998 of AIDS-related complications.

CONRAD R. PEGUES completed his B.A. in English at Memphis State University in 1991. He graduated with an M.A. from Memphis State in May 1993, also in English. "I'm at a place in my life where I'm trying to redefine my sexuality in relation to my race and gender without compromising either. I'm about revisioning what it means to be homosexual and lift homosexuality to a spiritual plane where it can be woven into the lives of black homosexual men and the black community as a whole without the trauma of rejection.

"I chose the Egyptian myth of the god Set's murder of his brother Osiris as a context in which to give voice to black homosexual men who often find themselves psychically mutilated by black heterosexual men."

Pegues lives in Memphis, Tennessee.

MARK HAILE, is an African-born American of African descent. He is a senior editor at the BLK Publishing Company, where he edits *Kuumba*, the black gay and lesbian poetry journal. He is also the author of the *BLK Guide to Southern California*. His articles, poetry, and prose are included in the books *The Big Gay Book*, *Blood Whispers*, *The Road Before Us: 100 Gay Black Poets*, *Sojourner: Black Gay Voices in the Age of AIDS*, *Sundays at Seven*, and *Uncommon Heroes*. His play, *Angelenos Anonymous*, was presented in the spring of 1993 on the anniversary of the L.A. riots. He is currently the literary events coordinator at A Different Light bookstore in West Hollywood. He lives in Chinatown Heights overlooking downtown Los Angeles.

BRUCE MORROW 's writing has appeared in *Callaloo: A Journal of African-American and African Arts and Letters* and *The New York Times*. He is the coeditor of *Shade: An Anthology of Fiction by Gay Men of African Descent* (Avon Books, 1996). Morrow lives in New York City.

DAVID FRECHETTE was a New York–based journalist, poet, and short-story writer. His essays, reviews, and interviews appeared in the *City Sun*, *Penthouse*, the *New York Native*, *The Advocate*, *Essence*, and the *Amsterdam News*, among other publications. His poems and short stories have appeared in *RFD*, *In Your Face*, the *Pyramid Periodical*, *Out/Look*, *Brother to Brother*, *The Road Before Us*, and *Here to Dare*.
    Frechette died of AIDS-related complications in 1991.

FABIAN THOMAS is English by birth, Jamaican by nationality, New Yorker by immigration, and fierce by design. He is an AIDS educator as well as a writer, poet, actor, and director. He is a founding member of the Brother Tongue Collective, a performance group. His work has been published in *Sojourner: Black Gay Voices in the Age of AIDS* (Other Countries Press, 1993).

CARY ALAN JOHNSON is an author, activist, and Africanist. His work has appeared in *Here to Dare: 10 Gay Black Poets* (Galiens Press, 1992), *Brother to Brother* (Alyson, 1991), *Sojourner* (Other Countries Press, 1993), and *Gay Travels: A Literary Companion*

(Whereabouts Press, 1998). He currently resides in Brooklyn, New York.

LAWRENCE DEWYATT ABRAMS has had his creative work appear in the *Pyramid Periodical, The Road Before Us: 100 Gay Black Poets,* and *Black/Out.* He was born in Harlem, where he currently resides, and is a graduate of Yale University.

LYNWOODT JENKINS, a native of Chicago, currently resides in Atlanta, where he has written and produced three professional stage plays: *At the Crossroads* in 1993, *Blackberries* in 1994, and *The Mustard Seed* in 1995. He also serves as the Atlanta correspondent for *SBC* magazine. Working occasionally as an actor, Jenkins is a regular performance poet in the Atlanta black gay poetry scene. Currently he is working on a novel as well as preparing for a one-man show entitled *A Day in the Life.*

ESSEX HEMPHILL was revered by many in the black gay community and was considered the foremost black gay poet in America. Hemphill's works were widely anthologized, and he was the recipient of numerous awards, including the National Library Association's New Authors in Poetry award for his book of prose and poetry, *Ceremonies* (Plume) and a Lambda Literary Award for *Brother to Brother: New Writing by Black Gay Men* (Alyson), which he edited. He also appeared in the late filmmaker Marlon Riggs's controversial PBS documentary on black gay life, *Tongues Untied.*

He died of AIDS-related complications in 1995.

RODNEY CHRISTOPHER is a writer living in New York City and has written for *BLK* magazine, a national monthly newsmagazine for black gay men and lesbians, and *Soap Opera Weekly.* He is also a contributor of the anthology *Boys Like Us: Gay Writers Tell Their Coming Out Stories,* edited by Patrick Merla (Avon Books).

CHARLES MICHAEL SMITH is a freelance journalist living in New York City. He has written for numerous publications, among them are the *New York Amsterdam News,* the *New York*

Native, the *Philadelphia Gay News*, the *Baltimore Evening Sun*, *USA Today*, *the Manhattan Spirit*, the *Lambda Book Report*, *Whazzup!*, and *QW* magazine. He was a contributor to *In the Life: A Black Gay Anthology*, edited by Joseph Beam (Alyson, 1986).

COPYRIGHT NOTICES